All my cash is tied up in debts

Canada in the Atlantic Economy

CANADA IN THE ATLANTIC ECONOMY

Published:

Forthcoming:

Other studies to be published later in the series will deal with policies for the transitional period and problems of harmonizing customs practices, transport policies, etc. There will also be a summary study in which the implications of the more specialized studies will be drawn together in an assessment of the over-all impact of trade liberalization on the Canadian economy.

Trade Liberalization and Canadian Agriculture

Gerald I. Trant
David L. MacFarlane and Lewis A. Fischer

Published for the
Private Planning Association of Canada by University of Toronto Press

To William B. Lambert

These studies of "Canada in the Atlantic Economy" are dedicated with respect and gratitude to the late William B. Lambert, Chairman of the Board of the Private Planning Association of Canada from 1965 to 1967, who played a vital role in the development and supervision of the Atlantic Economic Studies Program, on which the publications are based.

His interest went far beyond his formal responsibility; he held a deep conviction concerning the importance of international cooperation among the North Atlantic nations. His untimely death came when the first draft studies had entered the early stages of publication.

© University of Toronto Press 1968 / Printed in Canada / SBN 8020 3209 5

Foreword

There have been two outstanding developments in international trade policy during the past twenty years—the multilateral dismantling of trade barriers under the General Agreement on Tariffs and Trade, which has been the agency for several rounds of successful tariff negotiations since its inception in 1947, and the establishment of the European Economic Community and the European Free Trade Association in the late 1950s. In a period of reconstruction and then sustained growth, these policies have helped the participating nations of the Atlantic area to experience the benefits of international specialization and expanding trade. The wealth generated by trade and domestic prosperity has also made possible external aid programs to assist economic growth in the developing countries.

Whatever the trade and economic development problems of the future, it is widely acknowledged that the industrially advanced countries of the North Atlantic region must play an important role. It is also generally conceded that the ability of these countries to maintain their own economic growth and prosperity and to contribute to that of the less advanced nations will be greatly enhanced if they can reduce or remove the remaining trade barriers among themselves. Cooperation among Atlantic countries is now fostered by the GATT and by the Organisation for Economic Co-operation and Development. But the success of these and other approaches depends on the assessment by each country of the importance of international trade liberalization and policy coordination for its domestic economy and other national interests. This is particularly true for countries such as Canada which are heavily dependent upon export markets.

The Atlantic Economic Studies Program of the Private Planning Association of Canada was initiated to study the implications for Canada of trade liberalization and closer economic integration among the nations bordering the North Atlantic. It is planned to issue at least twelve paperbound volumes, incorporating over twenty studies by leading Canadian and foreign economists. Despite the technical nature of much of the subject matter, the studies have been written in language designed to appeal to the non-professional reader.

The directors and staff of the Private Planning Association wish to acknowledge the financial support which made this project possible—a grant from the Ford Foundation and the contributions of members of the Association. They are also appreciative of the help that has been provided by very many individuals in the preparation and review of all the studies—in discussions and correspondence with authors, at the Association's November, 1966, conference on "Canada and the Atlantic Economy," and on other occasions.

H. E. ENGLISH
Director of Research
Atlantic Economic Studies Program

Contents

The Impact of Trade Liberalization on Canadian Agriculture

Gerald I. Trant

I. Introduction

When relative costs differ among nations, the law of comparative advantage implies that real incomes may be increased by trade. The present paper examines, first, Canada's comparative advantage in agricultural production in an aggregate sense and, subsequently, the ability of Canadian farmers to compete with those of other nations in the production of particular agricultural products. The estimates of Canada's economic competitiveness for individual products are essentially estimates of absolute advantage, although, when considered together, they may serve as a basis for determining comparative advantage.

This study is essentially limited to an analysis of the competitive factors in agriculture itself. For the purpose, it has seemed advisable to make certain assumptions about variables of economic significance, of which the more important are

1. that international exchange rates, particularly between Canada and the United States, remain stable;
2. that there will be no major changes in production techniques in agriculture (a change of the magnitude of the conversion from horse power to tractor power, for example);
3. that intranational institutional arrangements will remain relatively unchanged;
4. that there will be no major changes in consumer preferences for agricultural products.

The ability to make distinctions, with greater or less precision, as to whether Canada will maintain an absolute advantage or disadvantage in the production of a particular product, depended not only on the assumptions made above, but also on fundamental economic interrelationships and adequacy of data. Data availability and completeness ranged from excellent in the case of wheat and coarse grains to very poor for greenhouse production. However, the most serious gap in data was encountered for Communist countries, many of which are producers of temperate agricultural products. Therefore, inferences drawn from the study should be modified by these restraints.

Canadian agriculture has depended heavily on exports as a source of cash income. Table I indicates the importance of agricultural exports to farm cash income. Large exports have typically been associated with high farm cash income, and low levels of exports have tended to dampen farm cash income. For individual commodities, such as wheat and flax, export sales have been even more important than for agriculture in general. Although the value of Canadian agricultural exports has exceeded the value of imports for many years, there is no guarantee that this situation will continue indefinitely. In fact, Table I suggests that the export surplus narrowed in a disturbing manner in several years.

TABLE I

CANADIAN FARM CASH INCOME AND
AGRICULTURAL EXPORTS AND IMPORTS
(million Canadian dollars)

Year	Farm cash income	Exports of agricultural products	Imports of agricultural products
1950	2,158	818	604
1951	2,793	1,020	711
1952	2,864	1,220	564
1953	2,788	1,147	541
1954	2,378	853	594
1955	2,384	801	639
1956	2,647	1,013	690
1957	2,575	909	709
1958	2,855	1,034	683
1959	2,811	970	739
1960	2,854	909	747
1961	2,988	1,193	813
1962	3,186	1,157	857
1963	3,199	1,359	1,004
1964	3,464	1,702	1,047

Sources: Canada Department of Agriculture, *Canada: Prices, Policy and Trade, 1963–64*; and Dominion Bureau of Statistics, *Farm Cash Income*, various issues.

There can be little doubt that U.S. agriculture and agricultural trade have been dominant influences on Canadian agriculture. This can be inferred from Table II, which shows Canada's agricultural trade with the world in general and with the United States in particular. In products other than

TABLE II

CANADIAN EXPORTS AND IMPORTS OF AGRICULTURAL PRODUCTS
(million Canadian dollars)

Calendar year	Exports to		Imports from	
	All countries	United States	All countries	United States
1950	818	302	604	274
1951	1,020	383	711	340
1952	1,220	303	564	280
1953	1,147	298	541	263
1954	853	235	594	301
1955	801	183	639	316
1956	1,013	206	690	362
1957	909	239	709	373
1958	1,034	289	683	362
1959	970	217	739	389
1960	909	193	747	427
1961	1,193	225	813	467
1962	1,157	224	857	479
1963	1,359	223	1,004	514
1964	1,702	332	1,047	550

Source: Canada Department of Agriculture, *Canada: Prices, Policy and Trade, 1963–64.*

grains, Canada has exported to the United States a much larger share than Table II suggests. Little Canadian grain has gone to the United States, although grain exports have frequently accounted for nearly half of the value of Canada's total agricultural exports. Aside from trading with each other, Canada and the United States have been directly competing in world markets for many farm products (as will become evident in subsequent sections dealing with individual products). This is to be expected, since they share, to a large extent, similar agricultural resources and production techniques.

Given that the United States is Canada's strongest competitor in world agricultural trade over a wide range of products, a comparison of the two countries' respective agricultural productivity may serve as a useful tool to indicate their comparative advantages. Different measures have been used from time to time to estimate productivity in agriculture, of which some appear to be more useful than others.[1] To express comparative advantage,

[1]See, for example, G. A. MacEachern and D. L. MacFarlane, "The Relative Position of Canadian Agriculture in World Trade," *Conference on International Trade and Canadian Agriculture,* Economic Council of Canada and the Agricultural Economics Research Council of Canada, Ottawa, Queen's Printer, 1966, pp. 95–104.

a measure of productivity must reflect value of output in relation to costs. In other words, the ideal measure of productivity would be the ratio of value of output to value of input for the industry in question. Superficially, many measures of productivity appear to meet this criterion, but on closer inspection they fall short of it. For example, measures of labour productivity, such as gross domestic product per man-hour or per active person employed in agriculture, are ratios of total value of output to a single factor of production—i.e., labour. Since land, machinery, livestock, and other productive resources are also required in agricultural production, they ought to be part of the denominator in the ratio of value of output to value of input if a meaningful measure of productivity is to result. No measure of labour productivity alone will, therefore, be adequate. It can be argued that other measures of productivity which embody a ratio of total value of agricultural output to the quantity or value of a single resource are similarly inaccurate. On these grounds, one must also reject such measures of productivity as value of output per animal, or value of output per acre, etc.

Another way of measuring productivity is simply to use total values of output and then to compare changes in output among different nations over a given period of time.[2] This method has defects of its own. It implies that the values of inputs used in production either do not change at all over time or else change at the same rate for all nations during the time period considered.

While no measure of productivity is free from flaws, one type which appears to avoid some of the inaccuracies discussed above is the ratio of an index of *total value of agricultural output* to an index of *total value of inputs used in agriculture*. Recently, indices of this type have been calculated for Canadian and U.S. agriculture for the period 1935 to 1964. They indicate that, over the whole thirty-year period, there has been an average annual increase in Canadian agricultural productivity of 2.2 percent, while U.S. agricultural productivity has increased at an average annual rate of 1.6 percent.[3] Since 1946, Canadian agricultural productivity has averaged an increase of 2.6 percent a year, and U.S. agricultural productivity has averaged a yearly increase of 1.4 percent. This result stands in marked contrast to productivity estimates obtained by using ratios of total output to a single factor of production.[4]

Increases in Canadian agricultural productivity have resulted from the interaction of two forces—an increase in output and a *decrease* in the

2*Ibid.*, p. 101.
3I. F. Furniss, "Productivity Trends in Canadian Agriculture, 1935 to 1964," *Canadian Farm Economics*, vol. 1, no. 1, pp. 18–22.
4MacEachern and MacFarlane, "The Relative Position of Canadian Agriculture in World Trade," pp. 97, 98, 101.

inputs used to produce that output.[5] Agricultural productivity in the United States has also been subject to changes in output and inputs. However, in the U.S. economy the forces have tended to work against each other: increases in output have been produced by increases in the amounts of resources used.[6] This result is consistent with the view that, in the United States, agricultural production has increased chiefly in response to relatively high price supports; at the same time U.S. agriculture has been encouraged to increase excessively its factors of input. On the other hand, Canadian agriculture, with a similar technology at its disposal, has had to adjust to the forces of a relatively free market, with the result that surplus resources have tended to be squeezed out of Canadian agriculture.

In any event, it is critically important to observe that, although Canada's comparative advantage in agriculture has improved relative to that of the United States, similar gains in productivity might very well be possible for U.S. agriculture under a somewhat freer market situation.

It may be reasonably inferred from the above that Canadian agriculture has a head start over U.S. agriculture along the road to improved productivity. However, with a common pool of technology and free movement of many productive resources between Canada and the United States, there is little reason for believing that Canada's current lead would be maintained under free trade. A more accurate understanding of Canadian competitive strength in agricultural production can be gained by the more detailed examination of individual products that follows.

The commodity studies presented in this and succeeding sections examine agricultural commodities of economic importance to Canada, with a view to discovering how Canadian prices and quantities would be affected if barriers to international trade were lowered. Furthermore, attention has been directed towards changes of a permanent, rather than to those of a temporary, nature.

Many agricultural commodities employ common factors of production, and a good deal of primary agricultural output is used to produce secondary products. Consequently, this paper considers both direct and indirect effects of changes in prices and quantities and examines relative changes of prices and quantities within agriculture.

As an aid to analysis and exposition, it seemed useful, first, to select one commodity whose position under free trade could be established with a considerable degree of certainty and then, where appropriate, to determine the relative position of other related commodities. Wheat was selected as the benchmark commodity because of its great importance to Canadian

[5]Furniss, "Productivity Trends," p. 18.
[6]*Ibid.*, p. 21.

agriculture as well as because of the fact that international and domestic statistics were more readily available for this commodity than for most other Canadian agricultural products.

II. Grain

Wheat

This section demonstrates that Canada has a considerable absolute advantage in wheat production over most of the world's wheat producers and exporters and that, with the freeing of world production and international movement of this commodity, Canada could expect to export as much wheat as at present, or more, and at prices relatively higher than those that have been in effect in recent years. The outline of the case for Canada's strong competitive position in wheat is straightforward; in effect, the paper argues that Canada has the potential to produce large quantities of wheat of superior quality at equal cost to, or at lower cost than, comparable wheat from other regions.

Since the early 1920s, Canada has been a major exporter of wheat and wheat flour in an expanding world trade in this grain. From the twenties until the Second World War, Canada was the world's leading wheat exporter. Since then, the United States has taken over first place, with Canada as a very strong second, leading Australia and Argentina by a wide margin. Since the early 1950s, France has also emerged as an important wheat exporter of about the same size as Argentina (Table III).

Although Canada has been delivering a declining percentage of world wheat exports, total Canadian wheat exports have been maintained, and even increased, in recent years. While Table III indicates that Canada has maintained a relatively strong position in world wheat trade, it also suggests that this country has been losing ground to the United States in wheat exports. The data of Table III, however, give only a partial view of Canada's competitiveness in wheat deliveries vis-à-vis the United States. A considerable portion of U.S. wheat exports in recent years has been of a non-commercial nature, involving a large degree of subsidy in price or terms of sale. These non-commercial exports have obscured the true competitive relationship between Canada and the United States in wheat production. A more accurate view of Canada's competitive position may be secured by comparing Canadian wheat exports with commercial U.S. wheat exports in recent years. It has been noted by J. M. Stam that, during the periods 1951–54, 1955–60, and 1961–63, commercial U.S. exports averaged 100 million bushels per year less than average yearly Canadian

TABLE III

WHEAT AND WHEAT FLOUR: WORLD EXPORTS, PRINCIPAL COUNTRIES

Year (beginning July)	Argentina Quantity (million bushels)	Argentina % of world total	Australia Quantity (million bushels)	Australia % of world total	Canada Quantity (million bushels)	Canada % of world total	France Quantity (million bushels)	France % of world total	United States* Quantity (million bushels)	United States* % of world total	World total (million bushels)
1920–29†	154	18.4	89	10.5	267	31.8			222	26.4	840
1930–39†	130	18.3	114	16.1	201	28.3			75	10.6	710
1945–49†	76	8.7	83	9.4	252	28.7			415	47.3	878
1952	29	3.0	99	10.0	392	39.7			317	32.1	987
1954	132	13.6	93	9.6	253	26.1	88	9.1	274	28.2	971
1956	98	7.4	126	9.5	282	21.2	14	1.1	549	41.3	1,328
1958	103	7.8	75	5.7	300	22.7	38	2.9	443	33.5	1,321
1960	70	4.4	183	11.6	343	21.8	57	3.6	662	42.0	1,576
1961	86	5.0	230	13.3	365	21.0	68	3.9	718	41.4	1,734
1962	55	3.5	200	12.7	320	20.3	109	6.9	615	38.9	1,580
1963	102	5.0	287	14.2	554	27.4	98	4.8	849	41.9	2,025
1964‡	156	8.5	238	12.9	435	23.6	169	9.2	718	39.0	1,840

Sources: 1920 to 1962 (excluding France): U.S. Department of Agriculture, *The Wheat Situation*, April 1963. France, 1954 to 1962: U.S. Department of Agriculture, *Agricultural Statistics*, 1963. 1963 and 1964: United Nations, Food and Agricultural Association, *World Grain Trade Statistics, 1964/65* (data converted from metric tons, wheat equivalent, at the rate of 36.744 bushels per metric ton).

*U.S. export statistics include 32 million bushels of wheat for 1963/64 and 35 million bushels for 1964/65 reported as shipped to Canada but actually representing only transit trade through Canadian ports and accordingly not included in Canadian import statistics.

†Averages
‡Preliminary.

exports.[1] In the same article, the author observed that Public Law 480 appeared to have more strongly affected U.S. commercial exports than Canadian exports, in the sense that the former declined more rapidly than the latter to countries where they were both in direct competition with PL480 exports. In point of fact, there is good reason to believe that Canada has shown a *long-term ability* to export large amounts of commercial wheat in competition with the United States.

Although Canada is sufficiently competitive vis-à-vis the United States in terms of quantity of wheat exports, its strongest advantage exists in the quality of its wheat. There are many reasons for believing that Canadian wheat has superior bread-baking qualities to that produced by any other major exporter. L. A. Fischer reports a ranking for wheat exports to the Common Market countries that places Manitoba grades 1 to 4 above all other grades and varieties, including Northern spring and Hard Red winter wheat from the United States, and Plata wheat from Argentina.[2] Other evidence indicates that, on the basis of protein and sedimentation, Canada's top four grades are better than top wheat grades from the United States and markedly superior to wheat from Belgium, France, Italy, the Netherlands, and West Germany.[3] Furthermore, Canada produces very large amounts of the top grades of wheat; for example, numbers 1, 2, and 3 Northern together accounted for more than three-quarters of the Canadian wheat crop during the five-year period 1959 to 1963.[4] A large number of countries import small quantities of Canadian hard wheat for blending with other wheat to produce a flour that is suitable for bread-baking (Table IV and Appendix Tables I and II).

Possibly the most compelling evidence of the high quality of Canadian wheat comes from the large purchases of Canadian wheat by countries that are net exporters of wheat. France has regularly purchased some Canadian wheat during the 1960s, despite the fact that it has been a net exporter of this grain for many years. Even the United States has made small but continuous purchases of Canadian wheat, other than seed, for domestic use (Appendix Tables I and II).

Sustained exports and a high-quality product are only part of the essential picture required for evaluating Canada's competitive position in wheat production. Although there might well have been reason for Canadian wheat to receive a price premium that would have been reflected back

[1]J. M. Stam, "The Effects of Public Law 480 on Canadian Wheat Exports," *Journal of Farm Economics*, vol. 46, no. 4.
[2]L. A. Fischer, *Future of Canadian Wheat Exports to the Common Market Countries*, mimeograph, Macdonald College, McGill University, 1964, p. 69.
[3]*Ibid.*, Table 31, p. 72.
[4]Canadian Wheat Board, *Annual Report*, various issues.

TABLE IV

PERCENTAGE DISTRIBUTION OF EXPORTS OF WHEAT AND WHEAT FLOUR
(WHEAT EQUIVALENT)

Exporting country	1959/60*	1960/61	1961/62	1962/63	1963/64
to Western Europe					
Argentina	41.1	38.5	59.7	47.7	17.8
Australia	25.9	30.9	28.6	16.4	14.7
Canada	59.2	53.6	46.9	46.4	29.8
France	41.8	46.6	47.7	22.2	50.4
United States	15.3	24.5	24.9	15.4	13.9
to Eastern Europe					
Argentina	—	—	0.4	—	7.9
Australia	—	0.6	—	0.5	0.5
Canada	1.8	4.9	7.6	5.6	13.8
France	—	1.9	—	19.3	19.8
United States	5.3	6.2	2.4	3.2	7.8
to USSR					
Argentina	—	—	—	—	4.0
Australia	—	—	—	—	21.5
Canada	—	2.2	—	—	30.8
France	—	—	—	—	5.6
United States	—	—	—	—	7.5
to North and Central America					
Argentina	—	—	—	—	—
Australia	—	—	—	0.1	0.3
Canada	5.8	5.1	4.1	4.6	4.8
France	5.2	4.0	5.7	2.0	2.8
United States	4.1	1.9	1.7	2.0	1.9
to South America					
Argentina	56.0	56.6	33.4	44.3	34.7
Australia	—	—	—	0.4	—
Canada	3.0	2.2	1.5	2.7	1.6
France	3.6	1.0	1.6	1.2	0.4
United States	12.7	9.9	13.1	13.2	9.6
to Near East Asia					
Argentina	1.4	2.4	—	—	—
Australia	15.1	9.6	4.6	5.4	6.2
Canada	1.7	1.5	0.7	0.9	0.5
France	3.0	1.7	1.7	1.4	0.6
United States	7.2	9.4	11.5	7.1	4.6
to Far East Asia					
Argentina	—	—	3.7	5.4	35.6
Australia	43.9	49.7	57.1	69.1	50.9
Canada	24.0	28.8	37.0	35.7	17.5
France	2.1	3.7	14.6	33.1	10.1
United States	44.0	36.3	28.3	43.4	41.2
to Africa					
Argentina	—	0.5	1.7	2.6	—
Australia	6.6	4.8	6.0	3.8	2.6
Canada	4.4	1.6	2.1	4.0	0.8
France	42.6	34.7	27.6	20.3	9.6
United States	10.2	10.3	15.7	15.6	13.2

TABLE IV (continued)

Exporting country	1959/60*	1960/61	1961/62	1962/63	1963/64
to Oceania					
Argentina	—	—	—	—	—
Australia	8.0	4.4	3.6	4.3	3.3
Canada	—	0.1	0.1	0.1	0.1
France	0.9	0.4	0.9	0.5	0.7
United States	—	—	—	—	—

Source: International Wheat Council, *World Wheat Statistics*, various issues.

Note: Total exports of wheat and wheat flour for each country per crop year = 100 percent.

*July–June years.

to producers in terms of higher prices, such has not been the case. Basic producer prices have been lower for Canadian farmers than for virtually any other nation's wheat producers. Table V, in conjunction with Table III, strongly supports the contention that Canadian wheat producers have the ability to compete with the rest of the world's wheat producers. Total Canadian wheat exports have been increasing throughout the world, while basic producer prices in Canada have remained below those of other nations.

Instead of using basic producer prices to compare competitiveness among wheat-producing nations, some authors have calculated the cost advantage enjoyed by Canadian producers using producer prices for a given time in the past. Recent estimates of this type suggest that, during the 1964/65 crop season, Canada had a cost advantage of 31 cents a bushel over the United States, 22 cents a bushel over Argentina, and about 7 cents a bushel over Australia.[5] Such estimates for a single point in time, however, tend to reflect short-term supply and demand forces as well as more persistent ones and hence may be most useful as additional evidence of absolute advantage.

Canadian wheat production has varied considerably from year to year as a result of changes in weather conditions and changes in wheat acreages. Table VI shows that variations in average yield have been more important than changes in seeded acreage as factors in the year-to-year fluctuation. There has been a remarkable stability in the seeded acreage of wheat during the period under study; in no year did it exceed thirty million acres,

[5]MacEachern and MacFarlane, "The Relative Position of Canadian Agriculture in World Trade," pp. 34, 35.

TABLE V

BASIC PRODUCER PRICES IN SELECTED COUNTRIES
(U.S. dollars* per bushel)

Country	1960/61	1961/62	1962/63	1963/64	1964/65
Europe:					
Belgium†	2.56	2.56	2.61	2.65	2.65
France†	2.20	2.24	2.33	2.36	2.39
Germany, Federal					
Republic†	2.82–2.95	2.82–2.95	3.01	3.01	3.01
Ireland	2.27	2.25	2.25	2.25	2.25
Italy†	2.83	2.83	2.72	2.67	2.68
Netherlands†	2.33	2.31	2.31	2.53	2.69
Sweden	2.47	2.37	2.67	2.79	2.89
Switzerland	4.23	4.23	4.36	4.36	4.36
United Kingdom	2.02	2.02	2.02	1.99	1.99
North and Central America:					
Canada	1.30	1.38‡	1.38	1.38	1.38
Mexico	1.99	1.99	1.99	1.99	1.99
United States	1.78	1.79	2.00	1.82	1.30§
South America:					
Argentina	1.25	1.41	1.28	1.45	1.42
Chile	1.99	2.01	1.36	2.29	—
Asia:					
India	1.99	‖	1.99	2.14	2.14
Japan	2.84	3.01	3.18	3.26	3.41
Turkey	1.66	1.90	2.21	2.21	2.21
Africa:					
South Africa	2.19	2.21	2.15	2.21	2.30
Tunisia	2.72	2.72	2.72	2.72	2.18
United Arab Republic					
(Egypt)	2.11	2.11	2.11	2.11	—
Oceania:					
Australia	1.70	1.76	1.77	1.61	1.63
New Zealand	1.88	1.88	1.88	1.88	1.88

Source: International Wheat Council, *World Wheat Statistics*, various issues. These prices and definitions are used as a basis for government guarantees to producers and are not necessarily comparable between countries.

*Converted at IMF par values except for Argentina, Chile, and Tunisia, where the IMF exchange rate for the first month of each country's crop year was used. 1964/65 prices for Argentina and Tunisia are based on their devalued currencies.

†Intervention prices for August, 1962 (applying to 1962/63 crop year), July, 1963 (for 1963/64), and July, 1964 (for 1964/65), respectively, for Belgium and the Netherlands, for the surplus areas in France and Italy and for the deficit area in Germany. Prices increase on a seasonal scale to take account of storage costs and interest charges and refer to soft wheat of national quality standards in 1963/64 (except those of Germany) and of EEC standard quality.

‡On March 1, 1962, the price was raised by 10 cents to $1.50 per bushel, retrospective to the beginning of the Canadian marketing year.

§Does not include producer subsidy of nearly 40 cents (U.S.).

‖In 1961 the Indian government did not fix guaranteed floor prices.

TABLE VI

CANADIAN WHEAT PRODUCTION, EXPORTS, DOMESTIC USE, AND STOCKS

	Production					
Crop year	Seeded acreage (million acres)	Total production (million bushels)	Average yield (bushels per seeded acre)	Exports (million bushels)	Apparent domestic use (million bushels)	Year-end stocks (million bushels)
1940/41	29	540	18.8	231	130	480
1941/42	22	315	14.3	226	145	424
1942/43	22	556	25.8	215	170	595
1943/44	17	282	16.9	344	177	357
1944/45	23	415	18.3	343	171	258
1945/46	23	316	13.6	343	158	74
1946/47	24	412	16.9	239	160	86
1947/48	24	339	14.0	195	153	78
1948/49	24	381	16.1	232	125	102
1949/50	27	366	13.4	225	131	112
1950/51	27	466	17.1	241	148	189
1951/52	25	554	21.9	356	170	217
1952/53	26	702	26.8	386	150	383
1953/54	26	634	24.0	255	144	619
1954/55	26	332	13.0	252	162	537
1955/56	23	519	22.9	312	164	580
1956/57	23	573	25.2	264	155	734
1957/58	22	393	18.2	320	159	649
1958/59	22	398	18.0	295	168	588
1959/60	24	445	18.2	277	148	600
1960/61	25	518	21.1	353	147	608
1961/62	25	283	11.2	358	142	391
1962/63	27	566	21.1	331	138	487
1963/64	28	723	26.2	595	157	459
1964/65	30	600	30.2	399	146	515

Source: DBS, *Handbook of Agricultural Statistics, 1908–63*, and supplementary data from Farm Crops section.

and in only one year was it less than twenty million acres. Typically, seeded acreage varied less than 10 percent from one year to the next.

Since 1939, Canadian wheat producers have faced two major crises during which it became increasingly difficult for them to market their wheat; one of these occurred in the first years of the Second World War, the other during the early 1950s. The response of wheat producers to these two, somewhat similar, situations gives a useful insight into producers' reactions to the limited production alternatives available to them. Two large crops at the beginning of the war, without compensating increases in exports, raised wheat stocks to record levels. The government reacted by offering an acreage bonus for land taken out of wheat production. This bonus amounted to $4.00 per acre for land taken out of wheat and put into summer fallow, and $2.00 for land taken out of wheat and put into coarse grains or grass.[6] Faced with little prospect of delivering their wheat, producers reduced sowings of this crop by nearly six million acres. This cutback was stimulated by a twofold incentive: government compensation for reduced wheat acreage and the prospect of substitute income from coarse-grain crops. Stocks of wheat continued to build up as a result of a large crop in the 1942/43 crop year. The government became more concerned and made it abundantly clear that little would be gained from wheat production in the 1943/44 crop season. Canadian wheat acreage reached a record low in that year. This was compensated for, to some degree, by an increase in coarse-grain and flaxseed acreage. With renewed prospects of higher exports and increased farm deliveries to the Wheat Board, seeded acreage of wheat rose by six million acres in the next year. From 1944/45 until the end of the 1940s, surplus wheat production did not constitute a problem for Canadian wheat producers.

However, a second wheat-marketing crisis soon developed. A series of heavy crops between 1950 and 1954 raised wheat stocks to unprecedented levels. Above-normal crops continued until, by the end of the 1956/57 crop year, Canada was holding nearly three-quarters of a billion bushels of wheat. Since then, expanded exports (notably to the Communist countries) have reduced wheat stocks; but record levels of production have counteracted, and wheat stocks have remained disturbingly large. Producer response during the 1950s and 1960s has been particularly interesting. From 1953 to 1957, seeded acreage was reduced by an average of less than 5 percent per year; from 1957 to 1964, it increased steadily to a record level of nearly thirty million acres. It seems that, as marketing became difficult, wheat acreage was reduced only gradually, despite the large build-up of stocks which hampered deliveries from farms to the Wheat Board. This was in marked distinction to the response in the early 1940s, when wheat acreage had been cut back drastically and rapidly. The essential difference between the situation in the 1940s and that of the 1950s was that in the 1940s producers had received a bonus for choosing the next-best alternative to wheat production and, accordingly, had increased their coarse-grain acreage and summer fallow (Table VII). In the 1950s, the switch to coarse-grain production was much less pronounced

[6] G. E. Britnell and V. C. Fowke, *Canadian Agriculture in War and Peace, 1935–1950*, Stanford, Calif., Stanford University Press, 1962, p. 206.

TABLE VII

SEEDED ACREAGE AND SUMMER FALLOW, PRAIRIE PROVINCES
(million acres)

Year	Seeded acreage			Summer fallow	Total†
	Wheat	Coarse grains*	Flaxseed		
1940/41	28	13	–	17	58
1941/42	21	14	1	23	59
1942/43	21	17	2	20	59
1943/44	16	19	3	21	59
1944/45	22	18	1	20	60
1945/46	22	17	1	21	61
1946/47	24	15	1	20	60
1947/48	23	16	2	20	61
1948/49	23	16	2	21	61
1949/50	27	14	–	22	63
1950/51	26	15	1	22	63
1951/52	24	17	1	22	64
1952/53	25	17	1	21	65
1953/54	26	16	1	23	66
1954/55	25	16	1	26	66
1955/56	22	19	2	25	66
1956/57	22	15	3	24	65
1957/58	21	15	3	25	65
1958/59	21	15	3	26	66
1959/60	24	14	2	27	66
1960/61	24	13	2	27	65
1961/62	25	10	2	28	68
1962/63	26	13	1	27	68
1963/64	27	13	2	27	69
1964/65	29	11	2	26	69
1965/66	28	13	2	27	69

Source: DBS, *Handbook of Agricultural Statistics, 1908–63*, and supplementary data
from Farm Crops section.

*Oats, barley, and rye.

†May not always be exact addition of component columns due to rounding.

than it had been in the 1940s, although there was a marked movement
into flaxseed. This reluctance to change crops without a compensatory
incentive suggests that wheat producers have few worthwhile production
alternatives.

The reactions by producers to crises in Canadian wheat marketings
suggest that Canada's low cost of wheat production results from a lack of

good production alternatives. Canadian hard spring wheat is produced on prairie land that has very little rainfall; consequently, the alternatives to wheat production have been restricted to coarse grains, oilseeds, and ranching. Although coarse-grain production uses the same productive resources as does wheat production, an increase in the demand for coarse grains requires an increase of the grain-consuming livestock population. This is a difficult objective to achieve in the short run. Other things being equal, a large increase in grain-consuming livestock, such as hogs, will depress hog prices and subsequently drive down prices for coarse grains. Moreover, when wheat stocks are high, there appears to be a tendency to use low grades of wheat for livestock feed. This is suggested in Table VI, which shows high levels for "apparent domestic use" where year-end stocks are high. In other words, a build-up of wheat stocks depresses feed-grain prices to a considerable extent because feed wheat is a good substitute for other feed grains. Table VIII shows that gross returns per acre from wheat have consistently exceeded gross returns per acre from alternative crops. Assuming similar production costs, it can be concluded that it has generally been more profitable for the Prairie provinces to grow wheat than to grow alternative crops.

TABLE VIII

GROSS RETURNS, PRAIRIE PROVINCES, FIVE-YEAR AVERAGES
(Canadian dollars per acre)

Period	Wheat	Oats	Barley	Rye	Flaxseed
1950–54	29.41	24.15	28.50	18.62	27.96
1955–59	26.21	20.12	20.71	13.02	24.03
1960–64	36.81	29.68	34.12	20.15	31.70

Source: DBS, *Handbook of Agricultural Statistics, 1908–63*, and supplementary data from Farm Crops section.

In view of these considerations it can be inferred that the opportunity costs of wheat production in western Canada are low. A reduction in wheat prices would divert production to alternative, resource-competitive crops whose prices would drop as stocks increased. This, in turn, would reduce the prices of resources used in wheat and feed-grain production, provided wheat prices were to remain low for a considerable period of time. Farmers would probably continue to produce wheat as long as they expected to cover direct cash costs of operation, including their own wages. Their last economic alternative would be to use the land for range purposes. However, this would require a substantial increase of cattle to utilize the range.

Such an increase would be biologically impossible to achieve in the short run.

It must reasonably be expected that most regions growing high-quality wheat would face similar adjustments if wheat prices were to decline. Since Canada's strongest competitor for wheat, in terms of quality, is the United States, direct comparison between Canadian and U.S. spring-wheat production is relevant. Table IX shows that, until 1960, Canadian yields slightly

TABLE IX

AVERAGE YIELDS, SPRING WHEAT
(bushels per seeded acre)

Period	Canada	United States
1930–39	12.5	8.1
1940–49	16.5	15.1
1950–59	20.2	15.7
1960	20.9	20.2
1961	10.6	13.0
1962	20.9	26.3
1963	26.0	20.3
1964	20.0	21.2*
1965	23.8	23.5*

Sources: Canadian data: Dominion Bureau of Statistics, *Handbook of Agricultural Statistics, 1908–63* and the *Wheat Review*, various issues.
U.S. data: U.S. Department of Agriculture, *Wheat Situation,* various issues up to February, 1966.
*Adjusted to seeded acreage basis by reducing bushels per harvested acre by two bushels per acre.

exceeded those in the United States. Since then, the two countries appear to have had nearly identical yields.[7] The situations facing producers in the two countries have been significantly different. Canadian farmers have been faced with a lower wheat price than have U.S. producers and, on these grounds, have had less incentive to seek high yields per acre. Furthermore, their U.S. counterparts receive price supports on an acreage basis contingent upon acreage limitations. Under the Temporary Wheat Reserves Act, Canadian wheat producers also receive small subsidies, principally in the

[7]With relatively free trade in productive factors such as machinery, fertilizers, and chemicals between Canada and the United States, and land being the main fixed resource in wheat production, yield per acre is a better indication of productive efficiency than it would be for agriculture as a whole, as discussed in the first section of the study.

form of assistance of storage costs on excess reserves. Canadian railroads have made less obvious subsidies to Canadian grain producers in the form of statutory grain rates, which appear to be below variable costs.[8] Taken together, Canadian subsidies appear to be in the order of 10 cents per bushel, while U.S. direct subsidies on wheat exports are nearly three times as great. There seems little reason for doubt that, under relatively free trade, Canada would be able to produce spring wheat at a cost at least as low as that in the United States.

Given that spring wheat yields only about one-third of total U.S., but nearly all of Canadian, wheat production, Canada may be expected, under conditions of free trade, to expand its exports of wheat to most countries, relative to U.S. exports, by selling a product generally accepted as being of superior quality at an equal or lower price.

Communist bloc countries have purchased substantial amounts of Canadian wheat in recent years, thus relieving what would otherwise have been a heavy surplus position. A rising standard of living in Communist bloc countries can be expected to increase their demand for wheat to replace inferior bread grains in the diet. While one can offer only conjecture on this subject, it appears probable that Communist countries will attempt to become self-sufficient producers, and even perhaps net exporters, of wheat. However, since available evidence suggests that only a small region in the Ukraine produces a product whose quality is comparable to that of Canadian wheat, it seems doubtful that Communist bloc exports would pose a serious threat to Canadian wheat exports in anything approaching a free market situation.

Barley

Canada has exported barley (for feed, seed, and malting) and malt in widely varying quantities for many years. During the 1930s Canadian barley exports averaged fourteen million bushels per year. This level was drastically reduced during the first years of the Second World War but nearly doubled in the later war years. Between 1940 and 1959 Canada exported as little as three million bushels, and as much as 122 million bushels, in individual years. The late 1940s and the 1950s witnessed a drastic increase in Canada's barley exports (Table X). In the 1960s exports remained at high levels but declined substantially below those of the previous decade. Canada's relative position as an exporter of barley has shifted a great deal, as the above-mentioned changes suggest. During a

[8]J. L. McDougal, "The Relative Level of Crow's Nest Grain Rates in 1899 and in 1965," *Canadian Journal of Economics and Political Science*, XXXII (February 1966).

TABLE X

CANADIAN EXPORTS OF BARLEY
(million bushels)

Period	Amount
1930–39 average	14.0
1940/41	4.6
1941/42	3.0
1942/43	34.9
1943/44	37.2
1944/45	40.0
1945/46	5.1
1946/47	7.7
1947/48	4.3
1948/49	24.6
1949/50	20.8
1950/51	27.4
1951/52	73.5
1952/53	122.1
1953/54	93.7
1954/55	80.9
1955/56	68.7
1956/57	81.5
1957/58	80.3
1958/59	70.5
1959/60	63.8
1960/61	47.2
1961/62	42.9
1962/63	15.4
1963/64	46.9
1964/65	37.0

Sources: DBS, *Handbook of Agricultural Statistics, 1908–63* and *Grain Trade of Canada, 1963–64*; Canadian Wheat Board, *Annual Report, 1964–65*.

recent five-year period, Canada ranked second twice, third twice, and fifth once, among principal exporting countries. Other major barley exporters have been the United States, France, Australia, and Argentina; in some years, Denmark, the Netherlands, the United Kingdom, and Sweden have also been large exporters of barley.[9]

[9]United Nations, Food and Agricultural Organization, "Barley Exports From Specified Exporting Countries," *World Grain Trade Statistics, 1964/65* and previous issues.

During the last half of the 1940s, Canadian barley was exported primarily to the United States and to Europe; large shipments to the United States continued throughout the 1950s. While the United States has imported a good deal of Canadian barley in the 1960s, the amounts have been much lower than they were during the previous decade. During the 1950s, continental Europe's purchases of Canadian barley declined somewhat, but there was a compensatory increase in the United Kingdom's imports. At the same time, Canada developed a considerable export trade in barley to the Far East. Since the beginning of the 1960s, Canada has virtually left the continental European market, although exports to the United Kingdom have remained important. Exports of barley to the Far East have increased substantially, amounting to more than 40 percent of total Canadian barley exports during the first part of the 1960s.[10]

Canada's strong competitive position as a barley producer is implied by its sustained ability to export large quantities of barley to the United States despite a tariff barrier and regardless of the fact that *the United States has been the world's main exporter of barley* for many years. However, it would be overly optimistic to assume that free trade would immediately produce a large increase in U.S. purchases of Canadian barley. A major component of U.S. imports appears to have been malting-quality barley, the demand for which may be expected to increase only slowly. The dominant feature of Canada's advantage in barley production lies perhaps not on the demand side but on the production side.

A considerable change has taken place in the geographical pattern of barley production during the last thirty-five years. During the 1930s the Prairies produced about 72 percent of Canadian barley; by 1965, 94 percent was produced in the Prairies.[11] It is interesting to observe that, under conditions of relatively free movement of resources, barley production shifted from the east to the west, despite the fact that per-acre yields of barley were higher in the east than in the west. For example, from 1957 to 1963 eastern barley yields were more than ten bushels per acre greater than yields in the Prairie provinces.[12] While it is true that freight subsidies paid on feed grain transported from west to east increased western barley prices relative to eastern prices, a similar development in oat prices did not have nearly the same effect on regional specialization in oat production.

Barley competes for the same resources as does wheat, but its gross returns are less than those from wheat (Table VIII). In western Canada

[10]Canadian Wheat Board, *Annual Report, 1964–65*.
[11]Dominion Bureau of Statistics, *Handbook of Agricultural Statistics, 1908–63*, and *Grain Trade of Canada, 1964–65*; Canadian Wheat Board, *Annual Report, 1964–65*.
[12]DBS, *Handbook of Agricultural Statistics, 1908–63*.

it is grown in conjunction with wheat for two main reasons: one, to provide on-farm feed supplies, and the other, to provide an alternative source of cash income in case deliveries to the Wheat Board are suspended. The greatest force affecting acreage and production of barley has been the market outlook for wheat. When wheat acreages declined, as during the early 1940s and throughout most of the 1950s, barley acreages increased to replace the wheat. Increased wheat acreages in the 1960s have resulted in a decrease in the acreage of barley. This is shown clearly in Table VII.

To sum up: under conditions of free trade, greater export opportunities and higher returns from wheat sales would induce Canadian wheat farmers to expand production, or at least to maintain production at high levels. If wheat acreage expands, barley acreage contracts because the two crops are resource-competitive. In other words, free trade would tend to increase the income of Canadian grain growers through expanded wheat sales. However, this would increase the opportunity cost of barley production and, in consequence, lead to a relative decline in Canada's competitive position as a barley producer.

Oats

World trade in oats has been small relative to trade in other grains. The United States, Australia, and Argentina have been the leading exporters of oats in recent years. Canada, like a number of other countries, has been an important but erratic exporter of oats. During the past twenty years, Canada has sent nearly 90 percent of its oat exports to Europe and the United States and has imported virtually no oats since 1935. World trade in oats has been as variable as that in barley, with countries entering the world market as large exporters for a year, then dropping back to their previous positions.[13]

The Prairie provinces have been the centre of Canadian oat production virtually since the west was opened up for agriculture. However, between 30 and 50 percent continues to be grown in the eastern provinces.[14] Almost all the Canadian oat crop—which has always been very large, running a close second to wheat in most years and occasionally exceeding it—is used domestically for feed. Less than 10 percent is exported in a typical year.

In the Prairie provinces oats have been grown as a secondary crop whose production has been dominated by wheat. Increased acreages of wheat have meant decreased acreages of oats, as Table VII indicates. In the eastern provinces, with their cooler, more humid growing seasons, oats have retained a strong position as a feed grain.

[13]FAO, *World Grain Trade Statistics, 1964/65* and previous issues.
[14]DBS, *Handbook of Agricultural Statistics, 1908–63*.

Canada's competitive position in world oat production appears to be relatively strong, as suggested by Table XI. Despite a sometimes adverse price level and a small but important tariff,[15] Canada has continued to export oats to the United States, itself the world's leading exporter of oats.

TABLE XI

CANADIAN EXPORTS OF OATS

	Exports to	
Period	All countries (million bushels)	United States (percentage of total exports)
1945/46	43.9	35
1946/47	29.8	4
1947/48	10.2	22
1948/49	23.2	85
1949/50	20.5	89
1950/51	35.4	88
1951/52	70.6	84
1952/53	65.4	92
1953/54	70.7	94
1954/55	22.2	68
1955/56	4.1	52
1956/57	18.7	96
1957/58	26.2	83
1958/59	7.5	20
1959/60	6.1	20
1960/61	2.7	42
1961/62	3.4	36
1962/63	21.7	12
1963/64	18.2	9
1964/65	15.2	17

Sources: D.B.S., *Handbook of Agricultural Statistics, 1908–63*; and Canadian Wheat Board, *Annual Report, 1964–65*.

Under free trade, Canada could be expected to maintain its oat production in the face of foreign competition. However, Canada's improved competitive position in wheat production as a result of free trade would reduce somewhat the volume of Canadian oat exports, as western oat acreage would decline due to increased wheat production. On the other hand, in eastern Canada, where oats is mainly used as livestock feed on the farm where it is produced, oat acreage would probably remain unchanged, as it has for nearly twenty years.[16]

[15]The U.S. tariff on oats has been 4 cents a bushel.
[16]DBS, *Handbook of Agricultural Statistics, 1908–63*.

Grain corn

Corn is one of the few types of grains which Canada produces but does not export in large quantities. For the last twenty-five years Canadian exports of grain corn have been negligible; since 1915 Canada has imported a large proportion of its grain-corn requirements (Table XII). Nearly all these imports have come from the United States. In recent years, grain-corn imports into Canada from the United States have had to climb an 8-cents-per-bushel tariff wall; but despite the tariff, substantial amounts have moved across the border, particularly during the 1960s. On the surface, this suggests that the United States has an advantage over Canada in corn production. While this may well be so, a number of factors complicate the situation.

TABLE XII

CANADIAN PRODUCTION AND IMPORTS OF GRAIN CORN

Period	Seeded acreage (thousand acres)	Total production (million bushels)	Imports (million bushels)	Imports (% of total production)
1915–19*	235	11.9	8.8	73.9
1919–29*	239	10.2	12.1	118.6
1930–39*	158	6.3	10.0	158.7
1940–49*	261	11.0	5.7	51.8
1950–59*	442	25.3	8.5	33.6
1960/61	455	26.1	21.4	82.0
1961/62	400	29.2	29.6	101.4
1962/63	421	32.0	31.2	97.5
1963/64	500	32.8	23.0	70.1
1964/65	—	53.0	20.8	39.2

Sources: DBS, *Handbook of Agricultural Statistics, 1908–63* and *Trade of Canada, Imports by Countries,* 1963 and 1964. Supplementary data received through direct communications with Dominion Bureau of Statistics.
*1915–59 annual averages.

For many years, U.S. corn producers have received price supports by participating in the loan program of the Commodity Credit Corporation. The popularity of this program among farmers suggests that it has provided a good deal of actual price support. Further complications arise from the acreage-diversion requirements of the U.S. price-support programs. These stipulations demand that corn producers who wish to be eligible for corn price support divert part of their corn acreage to other crops designated to be of a soil-conserving nature. Such institutional arrangements make comparisons of corn-production costs between Canada and the United States poor indicators of absolute cost differences.

However, Table XIII indicates that for the past ten years, despite the price supports in the United States, U.S. corn prices have been below

TABLE XIII

CANADIAN AND U.S. GRAIN-CORN YIELDS AND PRICES
(prices in domestic currencies)

Crop year	Canada		United States	
	Average yield (bushels per seeded acre)	Average farm price (dollars per bushel)	Average yield (bushels per harvested acre)	Seasonal average price* (dollars per bushel)
1955	62.2	1.06	42.0	1.35
1956	54.6	1.20	47.4	1.29
1957	57.8	1.18	48.3	1.11
1958	60.3	1.21	52.8	1.12
1959	63.7	1.16	53.1	1.04
1960	57.3	1.23	54.5	1.00
1961	73.0	1.12	62.0	1.08
1962	76.0	1.20	64.1	1.08†
1963	65.5	1.37	67.6	1.09†
1964	80.2	1.25	62.1	1.15†

Sources: Canadian data: DBS, *Handbook of Agricultural Statistics, 1908–63* and supplementary data from Farm Crops section. U.S. data: U.S. Department of Agriculture, *Agricultural Statistics*, various issues, and *Supplement to 1964 Grain and Feed Statistics.*
*Obtained by weighting state prices by quantity sold.
†Preliminary.

Canadian corn prices by an amount roughly equal to the Canadian tariff and exchange. It could be expected, therefore, that under free trade Canadian grain-corn prices would decline to a level comparable to that in the United States. In addition, there is reason to believe that U.S. corn is differentiated from Canadian corn on a quality basis, in much the same way that Canadian hard wheat and cheddar cheese are distinctive products with specific markets. From 1952 to 1956, inclusive, Canadian grain-corn prices were below those in the United States; yet substantial imports of grain corn (three and a half to five million bushels) entered Canada each year.[17] This observation suggests that purchasers were willing to pay a premium for U.S. grain corn. Discussion with persons in Canadian corn-processing industries (such as breakfast-food manufacturers and distillers) reveals that U.S. corn is available in a wider range of grades and types and hence is more suitable than Canadian corn for manufacturing purposes.

However, in the agricultural economy of southern Ontario, corn has occupied a rather special place in recent years; and despite large U.S. imports, Canadian corn production has increased. New varieties and improved production techniques have raised acreage yields to levels which compare very well with those of other crops in the southwestern part of Ontario. A recent Ontario study revealed that corn tended to be more profitable per acre than other grain crops such as rye, fall wheat, barley, oats, and soybeans.[18] Since (with the exception of soybeans) these crops are substitutes for one another, a reduction in corn prices would result in an absolute reduction in other grain prices; but in relation to each other, prices would remain comparatively unchanged. Thus, under free trade, corn production may be expected to increase slightly or to remain at present levels, simply because it would offer the best returns among available crops to many farmers.

Canada's absolute advantage in grain production

Three distinct but related factors have worked together to give Canada an absolute advantage in its major grain crops—wheat, oats, and barley. First, there has been a low real cost of production of these grains, chiefly because the Prairie provinces have had virtually no short-term production alternatives. The next best alternative to cropping—cattle raising—offers substantially lower returns per acre, especially since the existing cattle population cannot be significantly increased in the short run. Other factors that have kept costs of grain production down have been the substitution of machinery for labour and the increasing size of farm units.

The second factor that has helped to ensure Canada an absolute advantage in grain production has been the high quality of Canadian grains. Good seed and cultivation practices (while not exclusive to Canada) and the favourable factor endowment of land and climate together produce grains that are of nearly unique quality. It is this special natural advantage

---

[17]*Ibid.*
[18]This conclusion is suggested by M. J. Dorling in a mimeographed release, "Grain Corn Acreages and Production in Ontario in Recent Years," University of Guelph, 1961; see also Department of Agricultural Economics, "Production Opportunities on Ontario Tobacco Farms," University of Guelph, April 1965.

that enables Canada to produce a distinctly differentiated product for export.

The third factor to secure Canada an absolute advantage in grain production has been the application of strict grading standards. This system has been so successful that it now serves as the basis for grading grains in international trade. The rigid enforcement of this practice has permitted the sale of Canadian grains by predetermined grades—an advantage enjoyed by few other countries.

III. Tobacco

Canada produces a nominal amount of burley and cigar tobaccos, but flue-cured tobacco has accounted for nearly 90 percent of Canadian tobacco output for the past twenty years. Ontario grows more than 95 percent of Canada's total output of flue-cured tobacco, which is largely used for cigarette production (Appendix Tables V and VI). As a world producer of flue-cured tobacco, Canada has taken third or fourth place after the United States, Rhodesia, and sometimes Japan (Table XIV).

TABLE XIV

ESTIMATED PRODUCTION OF FLUE-CURED TOBACCO
(million pounds, farm weight)

	1961	1962	1963
United States	1,257.8	1,408.4	1,329.1
Rhodesia	236.8	234.4	198.6
Japan	173.7	190.9	190.8
Canada	195.4	187.6	187.7
India	154.6	163.5	147.5
Brazil	128.8	93.3	121.7
Rest of world	822.1	943.0	1,036.6
World total	2,969.2	3,221.1	3,212.0

Source: U.S. Department of Agriculture, *Annual Report on Tobacco Statistics,* 1961, 1962, 1963.

The United Kingdom has long been the world's largest importer of tobacco, and the United States has been its chief supplier, accounting for nearly 45 percent of British imports. Rhodesia, Zambia, and Malawi together have accounted for 30 percent, while Canada and India each have had about 10 percent of the U.K. market. Unlike Rhodesia, which produces primarily for export, Canada consumes about 80 percent of its tobacco domestically and exports the residual 20 percent. Canadian imports have amounted to about 1 percent of production in recent years.[1]

Almost every country taxes tobacco at some stage between production and consumption, and quotas and other controls abound in the industry. Canadian tobacco production has been heavily protected from international competition by a tariff of 20 and 30 cents per pound on stemmed and unstemmed tobacco, with the result that Canadian imports have been very small indeed. Canada's chief competitors in tobacco production have been the United States and Rhodesia. The United States has been able to sell its tobacco at a higher price than Canada for many years. Canada, at least recently, has managed to sell at a slightly higher price than Rhodesia (see Table XV).

TABLE XV

TOBACCO PRICES IN CANADA, RHODESIA, AND
THE UNITED STATES

(U.S. dollars per kilogram)

Year	Canada	Rhodesia	United States
1950	0.89	0.97	1.14
1951	0.96	0.89	1.13
1952	0.92	1.10	1.09
1953	0.97	1.02	1.14
1954	0.95	0.99	1.12
1955	0.95	1.04	1.17
1956	1.02	0.85	1.18
1957	1.08	1.01	1.23
1958	1.04	0.94	1.32
1959	1.22	0.89	1.28
1960	1.18	0.88	1.34
1961	1.04	0.87	1.41

Source: Department of Agricultural Economics, *Production Opportunities on Ontario Tobacco Farms*, University of Guelph, April 1965.

Both Canada and the United States have had stringent controls on tobacco production for many years, such as acreage allotments or legal rights granted to farmers to produce a given acreage of tobacco. The allotment system has produced considerable variations in the sizes of tobacco farms between the United States and Canada. The average acreage

[1]Rachel Berthiaume, *Exports, Imports, and Domestic Disappearance of Agricultural Products as a Percentage of Production, 1935–1962*, Canada Department of Agriculture, February 1965.

allotment of Ontario farms has been about thirty-four acres.[2] However, the effective size of acreage per grower in Ontario is a good deal larger because many growers own more than one farm; in some instances, husband and wife own a separate farm each.[3] In the United States, the typical flue-cured-tobacco allotment has been three acres, while in Rhodesia, where no production control exists, the typical grower owns sixty-five acres for the production of flue-cured tobacco.

If world trade in flue-cured tobacco were to be freed and production controls eliminated, Canadian producers could be expected to enlarge their plantings in order to reduce unit costs. The same type of adjustment, although it might take a little longer, could be expected to take place in the United States. The over-all result would be a reduction in world tobacco prices and, in turn, a reduction of Ontario tobacco-land prices.

Even if substantial price reductions were to result, Ontario growers would probably maintain, or even increase slightly, production of flue-cured tobacco as long as prices remained above 35 cents. This estimate is based on a study which investigated alternative opportunities to flue-cured-tobacco production in Ontario.[4] The study found that grain corn and potatoes appeared to be the next-best alternatives to tobacco production. Since, as the previous section on corn indicated, grain-corn prices would be expected to decline under free trade, the opportunity costs of tobacco production in Ontario would also be reduced under free trade. However, since free trade would eliminate much of the protection which Commonwealth countries now enjoy, the United States could expect to gain more from free trade than would Canada and Rhodesia. The net effect would probably leave Canadian tobacco producers slightly worse off, with little or no expectation of increasing production of tobacco except in Ontario, where resources and skills have been developed.

IV. Sugar

Canada is largely a net sugar importer in world trade; more than 80 percent of its sugar is imported, usually in the form of raw sugar, which is domestically further refined. There are no quantity restrictions on sugar

[2]G. Klosler, "Opportunity Costs of Resources Used in Tobacco Production in Norfolk County," unpublished Master's thesis, Ontario Agricultural College, University of Guelph.
[3]F. A. Stinson, *Report of Ontario Flue-cured Tobacco Industry Inquiry Committee*, February 1964.
[4]Department of Agricultural Economics, *Production Opportunities on Ontario Tobacco Farms*, University of Guelph, April 1965.

imports. Commonwealth tariff preference rates, which apply to Canadian sugar imports, have been most pronounced in the case of sugar for further refining. At between 24 and 36 cents per hundredweight, they have been one-fifth to one-quarter of the full rate. Canada has typically imported more than three-quarters of its sugar needs from Commonwealth countries, in particular from Australia, Jamaica, and Guyana.[1]

Canadian sugar production has been confined to beet sugar. Table XVI compares acreages, yields, and prices in Canada and the United States for

TABLE XVI

CANADIAN AND U.S. SUGARBEET PRODUCTION AND PRICES
(prices in domestic currencies)

	Canada			United States		
Crop year*	Harvested acreage (thousand acres)	Average yield (tons/har-vested acre)	Average farm price (dollars per ton)	Harvested acreage (thousand acres)	Average yield (tons/har-vested acre)	Average price† (dollars per ton)
1954	90	11.10	12.06	876	16.1	10.80
1955	82	11.98	13.42	740	16.5	11.20
1956	79	11.33	17.33	785	16.6	11.90
1957	84	12.58	13.24	878	17.7	11.20
1958	98	13.55	14.47	891	17.0	11.70
1959	90	13.70	12.78	905	18.8	11.20
1960	86	12.76	14.36	957	17.2	11.60
1961	85	13.02	13.13	1,077	16.4	11.20
1962‡	85	13.06		1,104	16.5	13.50
1963	95	13.83				

Sources: Canadian data: DBS, *Handbook of Agricultural Statistics, 1908–63*.
U.S. data: U.S. Department of Agriculture, *Agricultural Statistics*, various issues.

*Years for United States relate to years of harvest but, for California, include some acreage harvested in the beginning of the following year.
†Prices do not include government payments under Sugar Act.
‡Preliminary figures for United States.

the decade 1954–64. In recent years, Canadian sugarbeet production has been concentrated in the provinces of Alberta and Manitoba, but Ontario and Quebec still produce significant quantities.

Sugarbeet production has been supported by the Canadian Agricultural Stabilization Board for a number of years by means of variable deficiency payments to producers, which effectively insulate Canadian producers from

[1]International Sugar Council, *The World Sugar Economy Structure and Policies*, vol. 1. London, Haymarket House, 1963.

world changes in sugar prices.[2] Although Canadian sugarbeet production has grown considerably in recent years, removal of price supports could reduce Canadian beet-sugar production drastically. Since, as noted in "Trade in Agricultural Products,"[3] the guaranteed price to sugarbeet producers was 100 percent higher than the international price, it may be presumed that other nations producing sugarbeets would encounter similar price, and consequent production, declines.

V. Oilseeds

For many years Canada has had an active trade in oilseeds and oilseed products; both exports and imports have shown a long-term upward trend (Table XVII). Until recently exports exceeded imports slightly, but this relationship was reversed in 1963 and 1964. Flaxseed, rapeseed, and soybeans, in that order, have been the main crops in Canada's oilseed trade.

TABLE XVII

CANADIAN EXPORTS AND IMPORTS OF
OILSEEDS AND OILSEED PRODUCTS
(million Canadian dollars)

Year	Exports	Imports
1959	78	71
1960	86	70
1961	89	89
1962	99	90
1963	94	97
1964	96	115

Source: Canada Department of Agriculture, *Canada's Trade in Agricultural Products with the United Kingdom, the United States and All Countries*, various issues.

Flaxseed

For many years, Canada has been one of the world's principal exporters of flaxseed (Table XVIII), which has therefore become rather important in western Canada, where most of the Canadian crop is grown. Since 1955, more than 50 percent of Canada's production has been exported every year, and in some years the proportion has been as high as 80 percent.

[2]*Ibid.*
[3]General Agreement on Tariffs and Trade, "Trade in Agricultural Products," *Reports of Committee II on Country Consultation*, Geneva, 1962.

TABLE XVIII

EXPORTS OF FLAXSEED

(metric tons)

Exporting regions*	1959	1960	1961	1962	1963
Europe:					
Belgium, Luxembourg	9,598	15,076	20,250	18,512	25,443
Hungary			1,436		207
Netherlands	8,700	12,007	11,949	8,922	13,997
North and Central America:					
Canada	319,095	368,521	351,917	292,486	293,065
United States	214,670	105,401	115,000	100,141	86,575
South America:					
Argentina		63,038	98,955	6,638	20,692
Brazil			4,491	6,957	24,511
Uruguay			5,474	27,327	1,639
Asia:					
Iraq	8,369	4,860	4,964	6,883	1,836
Nepal	4,380	3,889	5,361	3,503	
Turkey	19,985	7,814	584		
Africa:					
Ethiopia	10,378	18,825	16,434	25,908	
Morocco	2,564	10,169	2,179	2,326	1,831
Tunisia	65	1,027	1,427	745	574

*Countries whose exports exceeded one thousand metric tons in any one year.

Source: FAO, *Trade Yearbook*, 1960 and 1964.

As in the case of many temperate crops, Canada's chief competitors in flaxseed have been the United States and Argentina. Cost differences between the United States and Canada have been difficult to establish with accuracy because flaxseed has been under price support in the United States, while it has faced a 10-cent tariff per bushel in Canada. Table XIX suggests that, while Canadian prices, until 1959 at least, remained typically below those in the United States, yields and total production of Canadian flaxseed have been sustained. However, as with feed grains, costs of flaxseed production in Canada are probably predominantly determined by opportunity costs, particularly opportunity costs for the production of wheat. Table VII indicates that high wheat acreages tend to drive down flaxseed acreage and production, while low wheat acreages appear to have the reverse effect. Since, as Table VIII implies, wheat tends to produce a larger gross income per acre than flaxseed, increased incentives to grow wheat would raise opportunity costs of flaxseed production. Consequently, it seems reasonable to conclude that Canada's share of flaxseed in world export markets would decline under free trade conditions. In any event, the main products of flaxseed—linseed oil and linseed-oil meal—are being replaced by artificial drying oils and soybean meal, respectively. It can be expected, therefore, that the importance of flaxseed will decline in world markets with or without free trade,[1] unless new processing outlets are found to stimulate world demand.

Rapeseed

During the 1950s, there began a phenomenal increase in Canadian rapeseed production (Table XX), most of which has been exported to the Far East and Europe. Canada also produces some rape oil crushed from rapeseed, which is a close substitute for soybean oil as a human food. But Canada's rape-oil production is small relative to its output of soybean oil. Rapeseed meal, which can be used successfully as a feed for cattle and poultry, appears to be less satisfactory for feeding swine. Its use as a high-protein feed supplement is unpopular because of toxic side effects. Aside from the toxicity problem, rapeseed meal produces less energy and contains less protein than soybean meal.

Improved varieties, at some future stage, could make rapeseed meal more competitive vis-à-vis soybean meal. Until such time, it is unlikely that rapeseed meal will replace soybean meal as a feed supplement.

Canada imposes no tariff on rape oil in either its denatured or undenatured form. However, there is a Canadian tariff of 5 to 7½ percent on rapeseed, and of 15 to 20 percent on rapeseed meal. As suggested above, it is unlikely that rapeseed meal would enter Canada even without a tariff; hence it can be concluded that the Canadian rapeseed industry is operating under conditions approaching those of free trade. Consequently, given the steady rise of Canadian rapeseed production and given its leading position in world exports of rapeseed since 1957, Canada appears to have an absolute advantage in the production of this oilseed.

Soybeans

Soybean production in Canada has been confined almost entirely to southwestern Ontario. Before the Second World War, Canadian soybean acreage and production were of little significance, but since then they have increased remarkably (Table XXI). Domestic consumption, however, has outgrown production, with the result that Canada has been a net importer of soybeans since 1940. Interestingly enough, Canada also exports important amounts

[1]A. Burnett, *Fats and Oils: A Review of Recent World Trends in Production*, University of Guelph, February 1963.

TABLE XIX

FLAXSEED PRODUCTION AND PRICES
(prices—domestic currencies)

Crop year	Canada				United States			
	Seeded acreage (thousand acres)	Total production (thousand bushels)	Average yield (bushels per seeded acre)	Average farm price (dollars per bushel)	Seeded acreage (thousand acres)	Total production (thousand bushels)	Average yield (bushels per seeded acre)	Season average price* (dollars per bushel)
1940	382	3,049	8.0	1.07	3,364	30,924	9.2	1.42
1941	1,043	6,780	6.5	1.26	3,462	32,133	9.3	1.79
1942	1,536	15,470	10.1	1.99	4,698	40,976	8.7	2.36
1943	2,984	18,432	6.2	2.15	6,182	50,009	8.1	2.83
1944	1,217	8,882	7.3	2.52	2,887	21,665	7.5	2.91
1945	873	6,225	7.1	2.50	3,953	34,557	8.7	2.89
1946	886	6,774	7.6	2.99	2,641	22,588	8.6	4.03
1947	1,791	13,822	7.7	5.24	4,264	40,618	9.5	6.15

Year								
1951	1,159	9,478	8.2	3.90	4,116	34,696	8.4	3.72
1952	1,110	11,660	10.5	3.16	3,445	30,184	8.8	3.73
1953	956	9,748	10.2	2.44	4,759	37,656	7.9	3.64
1954	1,178	10,998	9.3	2.54	5,947	41,274	6.9	3.05
1955	1,836	18,990	10.3	2.77	5,148	40,415	7.9	2.90
1956	3,041	34,991	11.5	2.56	5,786	47,037	8.1	2.99
1957	3,486	19,205	5.5	2.53	5,481	25,113	4.9	2.94
1958	2,551	22,342	8.8	2.62	3,862	37,409	9.7	2.69
1959	2,052	17,191	8.4	3.06	3,268	21,237	6.5	3.00
1960	2,513	22,571	9.0	2.75	3,437	30,402	8.8	2.65
1961	2,086	14,478	6.9	3.32‡	2,975	22,178	7.5	3.26
1962†	1,445	16,042	11.1	3.35‡	3,087	31,952	10.4	2.84
1963	1,685	21,176	12.6	3.20‡				
1964	1,978	20,313	10.3					
1965§	2,239	27,954	12.5	3.20				

Sources: Canadian data: DBS, *Handbook of Agricultural Statistics 1908–63* and supplementary data from Farm Crops section.
U.S. data: U.S. Department of Agriculture, *Agricultural Statistics*, various issues.
*Obtained by weighting state prices by quantity sold.
†Preliminary for United States.
‡Average of western daily price quotations.
§Preliminary for Canada.

TABLE XX

CANADIAN RAPESEED PRODUCTION AND PRICES

Crop year	Seeded acreage (thousand acres)	Estimated production (million pounds)	Average yield (pounds per seeded acre)	Average farm price (cents per pound)
1950	4	.1	300	3.8
1951	7	6.0	925	3.5
1952	19	13.9	751	3.4
1953	30	24.6	832	3.6
1954	40	28.9	722	3.3
1955	138	77.9	565	3.5
1956	352	299.8	852	3.5
1957	618	433.1	701	3.2
1958	626	388.1	620	2.5
1959	214	178.0	834	4.0
1960	763	556.0	729	3.3
1961	710	561.0	790	3.6
1962	371	293.0	789	
1963	484	443.0	916	
1964	691	661.5	835	
1965	1,435	1,140.0	795	

Source: DBS, *Handbook of Agricultural Statistics, 1908–1963* and supplementary data from Farm Crops section.

of soybeans and soybean meal and oil to the United Kingdom. This trade is mainly a result of the favourable tariff arrangements which Britain grants Canada as a member of the Commonwealth. Table XXII shows the relationship of Canada's exports and imports to production.

Soybean production has at times received price support from the federal government, but realized prices have, in fact, been above support levels for the past five years. At the same time, soybeans, soybean meal, and soybean oil for manufacturing have all entered Canada free of duty. For all intents and purposes, therefore, the Canadian soybean industry—on the import side—has been operating under conditions closely approximating those of free trade. Table XXI indicates that acreage and production of soybeans in Canada have been well maintained during the past five years, which implies that, under conditions of free trade, Canadian soybean producers could well compete with the larger U.S. soybean industry. At the same time, however, it would be unduly optimistic to suggest any large or rapid increase in Canada's soybean acreage because suitable land in south-western Ontario is confined to four or five counties. The principal loss to

TABLE XXI

CANADIAN SOYBEAN PRODUCTION AND PRICES
(prices—domestic currencies)

Crop year	Canada				United States			
	Seeded acreage (thousand acres)	Total production (thousand bushels)	Average yield (bushels per seeded acre)	Average farm price (dollars per bushel)	Harvested acreage (thousand acres)	Total production (thousand bushels)	Average yield (bushels per harvested acre)	Season average price* (dollars per bushel)
1940	11	844	18.3	1.90	4,807	78,045	16.2	.90
1945	46	3,323	23.4	2.55	10,740	193,167	18.0	2.08
1950	142	5,993	26.4	2.09	13,807	299,249	21.7	2.47
1955	227	5,001	22.1	2.03	18,620	373,682	20.1	2.22
1960	257	6,631	31.3	2.25	23,655	555,307	23.5	2.13
1961	212	6,608	29.9	2.48	27,008	679,566	25.2	2.28
1962†	221	5,002	21.9	2.80	27,857	675,197	24.2	2.34
1963	228	6,976	30.2	2.87				
1964	231	8,030	30.3					
1965‡	265							

Sources: Canadian data: DBS, *Handbook of Agricultural Statistics, 1908–63* and supplementary data from Farm Crops section. U.S. data: U.S. Department of Agriculture, *Agricultural Statistics*, various issues.
*Obtained by weighting state prices by quantity sold.
†Preliminary for United States.
‡Preliminary for Canada.

TABLE XXII

CANADIAN EXPORTS AND IMPORTS OF
SOYBEANS AND SOYBEAN PRODUCTS
(percentage of production)

Year	Exports	Imports
1960	28	245
1961	55	201
1962	37	223

Source: Canada Department of Agriculture, *Exports, Imports, and Domestic
Disappearance of Agricultural Products
as a Percentage of Production, Canada,
1935–62*, Feb. 1965.

Canada from free trade would occur in exports to the United Kingdom,
which are at present greatly enhanced by the Commonwealth preference.

VI. Fruit, Vegetables, and Miscellaneous Products

Fruit

For reasons mainly of climate, Canada has been, and probably will continue
to be, a net importer of fruits of all kinds. While this observation needs no
explanation in the case of tropical fruits, it may require discussion where
temperate-climate fruits are concerned. For more than three decades,
Canadian imports of temperate-climate fruit (excluding apples) have
closely approximated total Canadian production.[1] With the possible exception of blueberries, which Canada has exported in substantial quantities in
recent years, Canadian exports of fruit have been small, amounting to less
than 10 percent of total domestic fruit output. At present, apple production
is close to balancing consumption, but with improved varieties and con-
trolled-atmosphere storage, Canada could probably increase its exports.

Fresh fruit entering Canada in direct competition with domestic field
production faces a differential tariff, which provides increased protection
during the Canadian growing season and reduced support during the
remainder of the year. Commonwealth countries are exempt from this
tariff; but they do not, in any case, ship significant quantities of fresh
temperate-climate fruit to Canada. Removal of this tariff could therefore
be expected to lower Canadian in-season prices for many fresh fruits and,
indeed, to lead to difficult conditions for farmers if regional "dumping"

[1]Berthiaume, *Exports, Imports, and Domestic Disappearance of Agricultural Products.*

were to be practised following "bumper" crops. The over-all volume of imports could not be expected to increase significantly, but it might rise by a small margin. Total Canadian fruit production would probably decline slightly under free trade, except for blueberries and, perhaps, apples.

Vegetables

Canada has imported vegetables, mostly from the United States, at about four times the level of its exports.[2] This statistic does not include potatoes, in which Canada has had a small export surplus.

Canada's vegetable production has been protected by a differential but moderate tariff. Under free trade many domestic vegetable producers would face conditions similar to those foreseen for fruit producers: increased competition from abroad, pressure on domestic prices, and "dumping" practices in response to heavy crops in the United States.

One of the little known features of Canadian agriculture is the green-house industry, which has shown a very rapid growth in recent years. Canadian greenhouse area increased from 3.2 million square feet in 1951 to 23.7 million square feet in 1963.[3] The industry has grown most rapidly in the production of vegetables, especially tomatoes, cucumbers, and lettuce in that order. About two-thirds of Canada's greenhouse industry is located in southwestern Ontario (mostly in Essex county). No protection other than that given to field-grown crops has been extended to the greenhouse-vegetable industry, but it has flourished. Today, it supplies a substantial share of cucumber and, to a lesser extent, tomato output during peak production months.[4]

Competition for Canadian greenhouse growers does not come so much from their rivals in the northern United States, but rather from field producers in Texas, California, and Mexico. However, provided high-quality production is maintained, there seems every likelihood that Canada's greenhouse industry could survive under free trade.

Miscellaneous products

For specific agricultural commodities, such as maple products, turnips, and clover seed, Canada has, in fact, achieved an export surplus which is large relative to the size of trade involved. These products would be expected to gain from free trade, but large absolute increases in exports (particularly in maple products) would be unlikely.

[2]Canada Department of Agriculture, *Canada's Trade in Agricultural Products with the United Kingdom, the United States and All Countries.*
[3]DBS, *Greenhouse Industry*, 1963 and previous issues.
[4]W. G. Phillips, "The Greenhouse Vegetable Industry," unpublished Ph.D. thesis, University of Windsor, 1961.

VII. Beef

Canada's international trade in cattle has included four distinct groups, each of which warrants separate consideration.

Beef cattle

For many years, Canada's chief export market for live beef cattle has been the United States (Table XXIII). Considerable numbers of cattle used to be shipped to the United Kingdom, but since 1939 shipments, if any, have been negligible. Canadian beef-cattle exports have mostly been feeders—calves or animals more nearly ready for fattening. However, from time to time substantial numbers of slaughter animals have been exported as well. At the same time, Canada has consistently imported a small number of live beef animals, mostly from the United States and almost exclusively for slaughter. Occasionally these imports have become large, as they did in 1959 and 1964, chiefly as a result of temporary shortages of Canadian slaughter cattle. Virtually no feeder cattle appear to have entered Canada. The usual pattern of Canadian trade in live beef cattle thus emerges as a series of flows across the Canadian-U.S. border in both directions, but predominantly from Canada to the United States, consisting primarily of movements of feeder cattle from north to south and of slaughter cattle from south to north. The two-directional flow is simply a matter of local supply imbalances, which are settled internationally rather than intranationally.[1]

Two main factors have tended to isolate Canadian-U.S. cattle trade from competition by other countries. First, livestock disease-prevention measures enforced jointly by Canada and the United States prohibit imports of live cattle and uncooked meat from countries whose herds are infected with foot-and-mouth disease. These regulations virtually eliminate commercial movements of cattle from Latin American and many European countries to North America. Second, imports of live cattle from disease-free areas such as Australia and New Zealand are inhibited by barriers of high-cost, long-distance transportation.

Both factors leave Canada with an absolute advantage in supplying feeder cattle to the U.S. market. Free trade alone would not greatly benefit any potential exporters of cattle, such as Paraguay and Argentina, unless accompanied either by substantial easing of U.S.-Canadian disease-prevention regulations or by effective measures towards eradication of livestock diseases in those countries. If the latter goal were to be achieved, free trade

[1]This has been, at least in part, due to the relatively low tariff—1½ to 2½ cents per pound liveweight.

might well lead to increased cattle exports to the United States and might divert some U.S. imports away from Canadian suppliers. Even in that event, however, really significant changes in the present pattern would be unlikely because transportation costs would continue to pose a problem for most exporting countries.

In any case, it seems unlikely that livestock disease-prevention measures will change or that potential exporter nations will solve their disease-control problems; hence Canada may expect to continue substantial exports of beef cattle to the United States. Despite tariff protection of 1½ cents or 2½ cents per pound liveweight in recent years, and higher rates previously, the United States has been a substantial net importer of Canadian beef cattle (Table XXIII). Canada's high level of net exports has been accompanied by an increase in the beef-cattle population (Table XXVII) and in the per capita consumption of beef in Canada. The only substantial reductions in exports of Canadian beef cattle to the United States in recent years have been associated with special circumstances, such as the Canadian wartime embargo on beef-cattle exports (1942–48), the outbreak of foot-and-mouth disease in Canada (1952) and the resultant U.S. embargo (1952–53), and the Canadian cattle inventory build-up during 1956.

With only a relatively minor tariff on beef animals it can be argued that the existing trading pattern between Canada and the United States is quite similar to that which would develop under Canadian-U.S. free trade. Removal of the tariff between Canada and the United States would tend to shift farming operations to wheat production, increase opportunity costs for range land and feeding grains, and decrease profitability of feeding operations. An increasing number of Canadian feeder cattle would be sent to the U.S. corn belt to be fattened before being shipped back to Canada.[2] If these animals were to be slaughtered and processed before being returned to Canada, this could cause an important short-term dislocation of resources used in the Canadian economy.

Fresh (chilled) or frozen beef

Canada's trade in fresh beef, as in beef cattle, has been largely confined to the U.S. market for reasons of cattle-disease prevention. Under special

---

[2]With present fairly high feed-conversion ratios in cattle, and in the absence of feed freight assistance, it is cheaper as a general rule to ship cattle than feed. If feed freight assistance were to continue in Canada, there is reason for believing that feed and cattle would continue to be shipped directly from western to eastern Canada. This has been discussed by A. Wood in the *Canadian Journal of Agricultural Economics*, Vol. XIII. Somewhat similar results have been presented by T. C. Kerr in "An Economic Analysis of the Feed Freight Assistance Policy," a mimeographed publication of the Agricultural Economics Research Council of Canada, Ottawa.

TABLE XXIII
CANADIAN EXPORTS* AND IMPORTS OF CATTLE AND BEEF

Year	Exports of cattle†					Exports of beef‡ to			Imports of beef‖
	Purebred dairy to all countries	All cattle to			Imports of cattle†				
		All countries	United Kingdom	United States		All countries	United Kingdom	United States	
	(thousand animals)					(million pounds)			
1940	23.0	233.8	—	229.5	.2	3.9	—	.5	10.8
1941	29.8	254.1	—	250.6	.1	7.9	—	.9	8.8
1942	34.5	215.8	—	212.4	.1	16.0	—	4.3	5.6
1943	57.3	62.7	—	58.6	.1	13.5	.4	—	6.0
1944	53.8	59.1	—	53.3	.3	107.4	98.1	—	5.7
1945	71.4	79.5	##	70.7	.2	194.8	184.4	.1	.7
1946	97.0	104.6	##	96.4	.5	138.2	123.8	.1	.1
1947	76.5	83.2		74.5	.5	51.0	32.8	.1	3.0

1952	8.0	15.4	—	14.1	3.7	68.1	63.8	2.2	22.6
1953	42.2	69.5	—	67.3	2.8	28.8	6.6	18.7	24.4
1954	33.3	89.2	—	86.8	3.5	22.6	8.2	11.3	32.4
1955	41.8	67.6	—	63.4	6.4	12.8	—	9.7	34.7
1956	48.4	56.5	—	49.4	9.4	18.6	—	16.2	39.7
1957	40.8	387.5	‡	384.1	6.3	55.3	—	53.0	54.0
1958	46.7	670.5	—	667.0	4.5	63.9	—	61.3	58.0
1959	37.1	342.7	‡	340.4	33.4	30.0	—	27.2	66.3
1960	37.6	272.9	‡	269.0	9.1	25.9	—	22.7	49.5
1961	44.3	503.1	‡	495.3	3.8	37.5	—	34.0	53.1
1962	39.7	492.2	‡	484.9	3.6	27.7	—	24.2	55.6
1963	34.6	278.6	‡	272.1	3.5	25.6	.3	21.3	63.8
1964	38.1	222.2	‡	214.4	36.9	42.8	.1	34.9	47.8

Source: This table was derived from a G. E. Britnell and V. C. Fowke, *Canadian Agriculture in War and Peace*, Stanford University Press, Stanford, Calif., 1962; and DBS, *Farm Livestock and Animal Products*, various issues.
*Includes exports to Newfoundland until federation with Canada on March 31, 1949.
†Includes calves, although in practice cattle accounted for all exports to the United Kingdom and most exports to the United States and other countries.
‡Includes fresh (chilled) or frozen, pickled in barrels, etc.
§Includes purebred dairy and beef cattle. Imports other than purebred were negligible until 1952.
‖Includes fresh (chilled) or frozen, canned, salted or pickled in barrels, edible offal of beef, etc.
#Less than 400 head.

circumstances, Canada has shipped substantial quantities of beef to the United Kingdom. Such shipments were made as a wartime arrangement and during the 1952 outbreak in Canada of foot-and-mouth disease, which diverted exports to the United Kingdom because the United States imposed severe regulations. Typically, Canadian beef has not been shipped to the United Kingdom because it has not been price-competitive with beef from Argentina, Australia, and other suppliers (Table XXIV). Fresh or frozen beef imports have amounted to between a quarter and a third of total Canadian beef imports since the late 1950s. At the same time, nearly nine-tenths of Canadian beef exports have been fresh beef, nearly all of which has gone to the United States.

TABLE XXIV

FRESH (CHILLED) OR FROZEN BEEF EXPORT PRICES
(U.S. dollars per metric ton)

Year	United States	Canada	Australia	New Zealand	Mexico	Argentina	Uruguay
1959	1,392.8	930.3	537.0	688.0	457.3	420.8	435.2
1960	1,335.5	869.2	649.7	620.4	514.3	445.0	412.9
1961	1,340.7	754.4	659.8	640.4	607.8	412.5	392.0
1962	1,510.6	835.8	644.9	612.2	756.5	351.9	360.9
1963	1,570.9	858.0	670.1	635.2	794.5	381.9	331.7

Source: FAO, *1964 Trade Year Book*, 1964.

Under free trade, Canada could be expected to continue to export some fresh beef to the United States. However, no clear-cut evidence is available to suggest that Canada has an absolute advantage in fresh beef relative to the United States.

South American countries, such as Argentina and Uruguay, enjoy a large cost advantage in fresh-beef production over Canadian and U.S. producers (Table XXIV). Eradication of foot-and-mouth disease by these countries could result in considerable exports of their beef to the United States and Canada, with a considerable initial dampening effect on Canadian beef prices. In view of the magnitude of the Canadian-U.S. market and a fairly high income elasticity for beef, long-term adjustments under the above assumptions would probably not depress relative beef prices much below the present levels, provided that per capita incomes in the United States and Canada continue to rise.

Canada exports virtually no frozen beef and imports only small quantities of it, chiefly from Australia and New Zealand. Available evidence suggests that these imports are primarily used for processing into meat products in Canada. Processed beef products are discussed in more detail below.

Processed beef and beef products

More than two-thirds of Canada's beef imports consist of pickled or canned beef. Australia, Argentina, Paraguay, Brazil, and Uruguay have been the most important exporters of canned beef to Canada in the last decade. Australian canned beef has been permitted to enter Canada duty-free. Although these products are classed as beef, they do not appear to be close substitutes for fresh beef and are more directly comparable to cow beef, which is used in the Canadian meat-processing industry. Since free trade in beef products already exists between Canada and Australia, there seems little reason for believing that Canada's import-export pattern for processed beef would change substantially under free trade with all nations.

Purebred dairy cattle

Exports of purebred dairy cattle have been the most stable component of Canada's beef and cattle trade over the last decade (Table XXIII). Most of these exports have gone to U.S. milk producers. Since there are no tariffs between Canada and the United States on purebred dairy cattle, this traditional pattern of trade suggests that Canada has an absolute advantage in purebred dairy-cattle production relative to the United States.

VIII. Pork

The international pattern of Canada's trade in pork and hogs during the past twenty-five years has been similar to that in beef. During the 1940s, as a result of wartime contracts and heavy supplies of feed grains, Canada produced and exported to the United Kingdom considerable amounts of pork (Table XXV). In the early 1950s, the pattern of exports changed abruptly, with a reduction in total exports of pork, accompanied by a switch to the United States as the main importer. Since then, Canada's trade in pork and hogs, like that in beef, has consisted largely of a two-way flow across the U.S.-Canadian border.

Canada has consistently exported, but not imported any, live hogs. Canadian imports of pork products have increased substantially since 1960, to the extent that, in 1963, Canada was a net importer of this commodity (Table XXV). The pattern of pork exports and imports between Canada and the United States has differed from that of beef. Canadian pork exports to the United States have been specialty products, which, in the 1960s, have sold in quantities of about fifty million pounds a year, virtually independent of the prices charged.[1] Imports into Canada, on the other

[1]These products have included back bacon and hams. The back bacon has been so well accepted in many parts of the United States that the term "Canadian bacon" is used to refer to back bacon of domestic U.S. origin in many of the northern States.

TABLE XXV

CANADIAN EXPORTS* AND IMPORTS OF HOGS AND PORK PRODUCTS

Year	Export of hogs† to			Exports of pork products					
	All countries	United States	Imports of hogs§	All products to		Bacon and hams to‖		Pork meat** to all countries	Imports of pork products‡
				All countries	United States††	All countries	United Kingdom#		
	(thousand animals)					(million pounds)			
1940	7.2	.3	—	353.0	—	345.6	344.1	7.4	37.2
1941	37.2	33.9	—	482.0	—	464.6	460.8	17.4	5.2
1942	6.0	.2	—	537.4	—	528.1	525.0	9.3	.9
1943	9.3	.5	—	587.5	—	563.0	560.3	24.5	2.3
1944	9.7	.2	—	717.8	—	695.8	692.3	22.0	.7
1945	9.2	.8	—	462.0	—	449.8	446.1	12.2	—
1946	7.6	1.5	—	300.8	—	289.3	286.0	11.5	.7
1947	11.2	3.1	—	251.2	—	235.8	232.0	15.4	5.9
1948	7.4	2.2	—	229.5	—	204.7	200.1	24.8	1.6
1949	2.3	1.4	—	77.9	—	67.1	65.6	10.8	5.5
1950	1.6	1.2	—	85.1	6.6	78.5	72.3	6.6	5.7
1951	4.3	3.9	—	33.0	22.2	6.1	1.9††	26.9	22.5
1952	.7	.4	—	32.1	22.5	3.5	—	28.6	4.7
1953	21.1	20.8	—	78.1	66.6	7.0	—	71.1	.5
1954	26.5	24.9	—	76.1	66.9	8.9	—	67.2	1.5

1955	8.9	8.3	—	80.1	69.6	10.9	69.2	.2
1956	1.7	.7	—	67.9	56.6	8.8	59.1	1.5
1957	1.9	.5	—	43.5	74.6	5.2	38.3	1.7
1958	8.1	7.5	—	69.4	60.2	6.2	63.2	1.7
1959	4.5	3.9	—	76.1	56.1	6.3	69.8	1.4
1960	6.8	5.6	—	73.1	47.3	6.6	66.5	17.7
1961	27.6	2.4	—	58.4	44.3	6.3	52.1	42.0
1962	4.6	2.7	—	52.3	46.3	6.8	45.5	35.7
1963	3.6	3.2	—	52.4	46.6	8.2	44.2	89.8
1964	4.2	3.7	—	59.5	51.2	8.2	51.3	53.9

Sources: Britnell and Fowke, *Canadian Agriculture in War and Peace*, pp. 458–9; DBS, *Trade of Canada: Exports and Imports*, 1940–59, and *Farm Livestock and Animal Products*, various issues.

*Includes exports to Newfoundland until federation with Canada on March 31, 1949.

†Includes swine for improvement of stock and for slaughter.

‡Includes bacon and hams, shoulders and sides; pork—fresh (chilled) or frozen, dry-salted, barreled in brine; canned hams; and pork content of sausage, beginning 1950.

§Includes only swine for improvement of stock, not classified separately after 1943. Imports (by weight) of hogs for slaughter averaged 120 thousand lbs. a year from 1900 to 1904, inclusive; 5.3 million lbs. in 1905; 6.6 million lbs. in 1906; less than 10 thousand lbs. a year from 1907 to 1930; and were negligible from 1931 to 1960.

‖Includes bacon and hams, shoulders and sides, cured or smoked.

#Includes exports to Northern Ireland and Eire prior to 1926.

**Includes pork—fresh (chilled) or frozen, dry-salted; bologna, beginning 1946; canned hams and uncanned cooked hams, beginning 1951.

††Exports to United Kingdom became insignificant after expiration of wartime contracts.

hand, appear to have risen during the same period, partially as a result of pork prices in Canada exceeding those in the United States. Another important reason for the expansion of U.S. exports into Canada since 1960 has been the removal of the Canadian embargo on uncooked pork products of U.S. origin, which had been in effect because of the presence of the disease vesicular entheme in the United States. Fresh-pork imports, which had not exceeded 10 percent of total pork imports during the period 1956–60, rose to a level of 80 percent between 1960 and 1964.

Relative to other countries, particularly the United States, Canada does not appear to enjoy any sustained advantage in pork production. On the contrary, available price evidence implies that Canada is a high-cost pork producer relative to many other important pork-producing nations (Table XXVI).

Under free trade, Canada could hope to maintain, or perhaps to increase slightly, its exports of high-quality specialty pork products to the United States. On the other hand, free trade might result in higher feed-grain costs for Canada because factors would shift into wheat production. Consequently, Canada's hog production costs would rise above, or at best remain at, present levels, and imports of pork (probably from the United States) might well increase.

IX. Sheep and Lambs

Livestock and farm outputs of sheep and lambs, unlike those of cattle and hogs, have steadily declined over the last thirty years (Table XXVII). Exports have also been diminishing and, since 1950, have amounted to less than 10 percent of production. Imports have risen from 12 to over 100 percent of production during the same period. Most of Canada's trade in sheep and lambs, as in other livestock, has been with the United States. Most imports of mutton and lamb, however, have come from Australia and New Zealand. Frozen lamb and mutton have been more readily accepted by consumers than frozen beef, leading to one of the essential differences in the marketability of these products.

There has been relatively free access for lamb and lamb products to the Canadian market—a tariff of half a cent per pound on lamb and mutton, and a zero tariff on wool in the grease. Free trade would be expected to increase slightly Canada's imports of lamb and mutton and to accelerate moderately the downward trend in the Canadian sheep industry. The latter development, in turn, would lead to increased wool imports to meet domestic requirements, even without a rise in domestic demand.

TABLE XXVI

FRESH (CHILLED) OR FROZEN SWINE MEAT EXPORT PRICES
(U.S. dollars per metric ton)

Year	Belgium-Luxembourg	Denmark	Netherlands	Sweden	Yugoslavia	Canada	United States	Argentina
1959	729.0	661.4	652.5	503.3	560.2	748.3	338.7	450.0
1960	566.2	579.8	660.8	478.4	572.4	690.1	538.4	497.3
1961	754.1	639.7	728.5	516.6	594.5	868.9	642.5	512.5
1962	642.1	644.8	669.4	515.0	676.8	833.5	633.6	595.1
1963	909.7	754.9	794.6	659.3	772.3	838.3	609.5	709.7

Source: FAO, *Trade Yearbook*, 1964.

TABLE XXVII

LIVESTOCK AND FARM OUTPUT* OF CATTLE, HOGS, AND SHEEP AND LAMBS IN CANADA
(thousand animals)

	Cattle		Hogs		Sheep and lambs	
Year†	Livestock	Farm output	Livestock	Farm output	Livestock	Farm output
1930	7,686	970	3,735	3,976	3,438	1,440
1935	8,973	1,388	3,651	4,720	3,224	1,613
1940	8,380	1,560	6,002	7,244	2,887	1,284
1945	9,632	2,478	4,964	8,718	3,032	1,578
1950	8,343	2,107	4,372	6,794	1,579	829
1955	10,603	2,330	4,800	6,941	1,634	745
1956	11,011	2,466	4,731	6,860	1,620	757
1957	11,265	2,816	4,758	6,297	1,628	752
1958	10,990	2,908	5,931	7,474	1,630	740
1959	11,058	2,454	6,519	9,666	1,608	735
1960	11,337	2,640	5,070	7,811	1,607	716
1961	11,934	2,852	5,331	7,550	1,548	773
1962	12,075	2,751	4,973	7,653	1,433	767
1963	12,305	2,821	5,210	7,605	1,340	660
1964	12,817	3,031	5,620	8,305	1,286	643

Sources: Britnell and Fowke, *Canadian Agriculture in War and Peace*, 1962. The figures are based on data from Livestock Section, Agriculture Division, Dominion Bureau of Statistics. (Data for 1930 are not fully comparable with the revised data from that year forward.) 1956–64 data: DBS, *Farm Livestock and Animal Products*, 1964.

*"Farm output" includes commercial marketings plus estimates of farm and local slaughter.

†For livestock data, "year" as of June 1st.

X. Dairy Products

Cheese

Canada had a well-developed market for dairy products, mostly cheddar cheese, in the United Kingdom from 1900 until 1946. With the termination of wartime cheese contracts, the United Kingdom sought dairy products from non-dollar producers and drastically reduced its imports of Canadian cheese (Table XXVIII). It is significant that Canadian cheddar cheese exported to the United Kingdom commands a premium over similar cheeses produced by other nations. For example, in 1964–65 Canadian finest white cheese sold in London at a premium of between 11 and 19 cents per pound over New Zealand finest white cheese and at a considerable premium over most other cheeses of comparable types from England, Denmark, the

TABLE XXVIII

CANADIAN EXPORTS OF BUTTER, CHEESE, AND CONCENTRATED WHOLE MILK PRODUCTS AND IMPORTS OF BUTTER AND CHEESE
(million pounds)

Year	Exports* Butter United Kingdom	Butter All countries	Cheese United Kingdom	Cheese All countries	Condensed milk	Evaporated milk	Milk powder†	Imports Butter	Imports Cheese
1940	.0	1.3	103.2	106.6	6.8	34.7	4.4	.0	1.0
1945	—	5.6	132.9	135.4	18.7	70.8	6.0	.0	.7
1950	—	1.6	59.2	63.1	3.9	33.6	9.2	.0	10.2
1955	.0	7.4	12.6	13.7	1.3	5.3	16.1	.0	12.7
1956	.0	2.1	10.9	12.2	2.6	6.3	17.3	.0	9.0
1957	—	.0	7.5	8.5	.7	4.6	16.4	.0	9.4
1958	—	.0	14.9	15.7	—	3.2	17.5	.0	11.2
1959	10.5	10.5	19.2	20.0	—	5.0	18.4	.0	13.0
1960	2.9	3.0	17.7	18.8	—	3.3	36.7	.0	13.2
1961	—	.0	18.3	19.5	—	4.7	25.8	—‡	14.7
1962	—	.0	26.1	27.3	—	6.1	20.2	—	14.6
1963	5.6	5.6	24.6	25.8	—	5.9	17.1	—	15.4
1964	36.5	113.7	30.0	31.7	—	18.1	18.4	—	15.3

Source: Britnell and Fowke, *Canadian Agriculture in War and Peace*, p. 463.
*Includes exports to Newfoundland until federation with Canada on March 31, 1949.
†Whole milk powder.
‡Less than 500 lbs.

Netherlands, and West Germany. However, it would be incorrect to infer on the basis of this premium price that Canada has an absolute advantage in cheese production. New Zealand's exports of cheese have been, in a typical year, about ten times as large, and Denmark's about eight times as large, as Canada's exports. The Netherlands has exported even more (Table XXIX). Since these nations have consistently been exporting cheese in large quantities at prices substantially below Canada's (Table XXX), they appear to have an absolute advantage over Canada in cheese production. While Canada does enjoy the advantage of exporting a specialized, differentiated product, the market for that product appears to be fairly limited. There is little reason to assume that exports of Canadian cheddar

TABLE XXIX

EXPORTS OF CHEESE AND CURD
(metric tons)

Exporting region*	1959	1960	1961	1962	1963
Europe:					
Austria	7,177	6,056	6,986	8,063	9,276
Belgium-Luxembourg	416	775	2,060	6,311	4,563
Bulgaria	6,944	8,759	10,694	10,495	3,951
Denmark	79,015	75,925	78,972	81,455	78,913
Finland	17,852	16,962	17,793	16,860	17,263
France	28,210	31,261	39,349	36,199	45,476
Germany, Fed. Rep.	8,862	12,178	11,835	18,054	18,923
Hungary	5,563	5,965	7,783	7,510	8,824
Ireland	754	754	2,370	4,397	6,904
Italy	21,397	23,454	23,181	26,671	25,651
Netherlands	105,580	109,152	107,901	109,187	117,517
Norway	9,700	10,366	9,502	9,536	13,833
Poland	4,984	6,431	3,590	1,892	1,221
Sweden	3,997	3,209	3,399	5,536	6,682
Switzerland	28,787	31,057	33,356	32,317	33,731
United Kingdom	2,472	3,112	2,979	2,868	2,716
North America:					
Canada	9,076	8,554	8,862	12,370	11,721
United States†	6,428	4,236	4,118	3,286	15,374
South America:					
Argentina	3,441	3,084	3,882	3,924	5,412
Oceania:					
Australia	14,642	19,230	18,326	22,737	26,356
New Zealand	84,790	80,686	89,011	93,774	92,015

Source: FAO, *Trade Yearbook*, 1960 and 1964.
*Countries whose exports exceeded 5,000 metric tons in any one year.
†Includes re-exports.

TABLE XXX

EXPORT AND IMPORT VALUES OF CHEESE AND CURD, SELECTED COUNTRIES
(U.S. dollars per metric ton)

Country	1959	1960	1961	1962	1963
Exports					
Denmark	603.32	610.30	613.84	613.57	665.37
France	987.10	1,026.07	929.60	947.32	862.48
Italy	1,131.33	1,253.05	1,190.59	1,137.00	1,224.40
Netherlands	619.48	567.57	601.04	598.89	595.88
Switzerland	1,110.36	1,123.06	1,303.27	1,130.71	1,173.25
Canada	834.51	783.61	706.27	672.92	715.89
United States	875.93	1,013.03	1,153.75	1,080.48	697.38
Australia	683.38	581.18	563.19	512.60	517.98
New Zealand	729.90	644.00	625.61	555.77	548.89
Imports					
Belgium-Luxembourg	713.62	694.48	724.24	739.14	776.31
France	937.15	1,001.48	1,099.51	1,012.50	1,077.43
Germany, Fed. Rep.	567.87	555.83	606.01	594.01	615.29
Italy	825.43	827.66	795.51	773.70	793.18
United Kingdom	776.11	670.42	644.79	650.95	658.43
Canada	1,062.63	1,125.46	1,113.46	1,073.42	1,081.22
United States	1,065.01	1,092.66	1,035.16	1,032.38	989.19

Source: FAO, *Trade Yearbook*, 1964.

cheese to the United Kingdom could expand by a large amount without an accompanying reduction in price. Canada's trade in cheese with the United Kingdom is already in fairly free competition with that of New Zealand and other Commonwealth countries; and under free trade, Canadian cheddar cheese exports and premium prices would be expected to remain approximately at present levels.

Canada exports significant quantities of cheddar cheese but consumes most of its production domestically. Increasing amounts of specialty cheeses have entered Canada since 1950 (Table XXVIII), most of which have faced a substantial tariff if imported from non-Commonwealth countries. There is little doubt that in the short run, zero tariffs would lead to a significant increase in Canadian imports of specialty cheeses.

Butter

Canada is not an important world exporter of butter (Table XXXI) and consumes most of its butter production domestically. As Table XXVIII suggests, Canada has had a virtual embargo on butter for many years. In the interest of domestic products, it has not imported any butter since 1953. To maintain domestic production at adequate levels, large price-

TABLE XXXI

EXPORTS OF BUTTER
(metric tons)

Exporting region*	1959	1960	1961	1962	1963
Europe:					
Austria	5,295	5,340	3,260	3,534	4,185
Belgium-Luxembourg	44	6,329	9,466	3,577	4,472
Bulgaria	2,187	2,570	1,704	1,791	761
Denmark	117,950	118,082	120,043	114,717	102,358
Finland	21,432	25,725	17,499	10,209	15,772
France	12,192	23,145	51,224	30,316	40,699
Hungary	4,964	5,723	4,008	4,663	5,481
Ireland	1,332	7,638	15,399	16,282	19,541
Netherlands	39,924	39,269	31,133	32,586	40,673
Norway	6,371	6,754	5,425	5,134	3,798
Poland	22,687	28,599	26,691	27,461	18,563
Sweden	4,211	11,833	8,572	16,954	10,608
United Kingdom†	2,481	2,717	3,252	3,129	2,033
North America:					
Canada	4,764	1,367	3	2	2,544
United States†	9,721	584	335	2,619	26,378
South America:					
Argentina	23,203	24,303	14,098	11,096	13,321
Africa:					
Kenya	2,597	2,506	2,185	3,392	2,963
South Africa	1,891	1,035	13,578	4,845	1,137
Oceania:					
Australia	79,720	79,355	63,823	80,789	81,133
New Zealand	196,073	159,569	167,686	171,139	166,726

Source: FAO, *Trade Yearbook*, 1960 and 1964.
*Countries whose exports exceeded 2000 metric tons in any one year.
†Includes re-exports.

support expenditures have been required (Table XXXII). From time to time, such price supports have resulted in surplus butter production in Canada, as in 1960, 1961, and 1962. Canada's absolute disadvantage in butter production can be most clearly inferred from the fact that New Zealand butter has been sold in large quantities in the United Kingdom at a price nearly 20 cents below the Canadian support price of 64 cents per pound. Even with price supports, Canada does not produce enough butter to be a consistent exporter. Free trade would undoubtedly increase Canada's imports of butter and force domestic prices down.

ASSISTANCE PAID ON (SPECIFIC) COMMODITIES BY THE CANADIAN GOVERNMENT, DEPARTMENT OF AGRICULTURE (thousand dollars)

Commodity	54/55	55/56	56/57	57/58	58/59	59/60	60/61	61/62	62/63	63/64
Hogs and pork*	6,041	5,886	5,698	5,442	7,202	38,005	35,610	8,732	12,906	14,185
Lamb					281	361	101		627	585
Fowl				154	423	138	†	1,423	663	10
Eggs	118	490	55	1,483	3,426	4,810	2,096	38	956	727
Wool				1,541	1,541	1,219	1,253	1,236		
Butter‡	1,790	5,303	4,711	2,777	342	3,409	2,442	2,482	45,239	108,957
Cheese§	719	596	641	845	1,523	923	1,122	1,549	1,950	6,162
Dry skim milk						8,108	7	100	1,052‖	1,168†
Milk for manufacturing				1,094	6,957	9,844	11,433	12,371	13,258	1,865
Whole milk powder for international relief									4,914	
Assistance to western grain producers					40,588		40,430	39,974	113#	
Other supports to grains	18,699	16,333	17,164	17,778	63,471	64,878	68,610	66,956	50,264	59,547
Potatoes	4,585	486	187	480	367			597	619	
Tomatoes					52	96	36			
Asparagus					106					
Sugarbeets						2,657	2,716	1,670	1,983	2
Soybeans						1,217	867			
Sunflower seed for crushing							44			
Apples	602		182		769					
Peaches						357	268			
Raspberries					*	31		7		
Honey								91	371	76

Source: Canada Department of Agriculture, *Supplement to Federal Agricultural Assistance Programme*, various issues.

*Includes hog premiums paid on quantity actually shipped and graded during the fiscal year.
†Less than $500.
‡Includes assistance to imported butter.
§Includes quality premiums.
‖Includes product for international relief and sale for export programs.
#Excludes $26,740 refunded from previous year's expenditure—provincial breakdown for this refund was not available.

Condensed milk and milk powder

For products such as condensed or evaporated milk and milk powder, too few data are available to reach definite conclusions about Canada's competitive position. Canada has, however, exported a small but fairly steady quantity of evaporated milk and milk powder for many years.

General trends

Canada's dairy industry has received substantial tariff protection, as well as direct financial support, for many years (Table XXXII). Despite such protection, dairy-cattle production has steadily declined in Canada (Table XXVII). Consequently, it can be inferred that Canada's dairy industry is at an absolute disadvantage in relation to other nations. It also appears to be at a comparative disadvantage relative to other lines of agricultural production in Canada. There can be little doubt that Canadian dairy farming would decline substantially under the economic pressures that would be brought upon it by free trade. The decline of the Canadian dairy industry might be somewhat mitigated by new sales outlets for fluid milk to large U.S. population centres such as Detroit or Buffalo. This possibility would depend entirely upon the way in which the United States decided to change the boundaries of the areas supplying milk to the cities in question. In any event, it is not clear whether fluid milk would tend to move from Canada to the United States or from the United States to Canada.

Any decline in the Canadian dairy industry would affect some provinces more than others. In recent years, the number of dairy cows has been increasing in the province of Quebec but declining in most others.[1] This has been attributed to the limited alternatives available to Quebec farmers, who have been faced with a short growing season more suitable for forage production than for grain crops required for the fattening of livestock. Consequently, while most Canadian dairy producers would be hurt by free trade, Quebec producers, because of their limited alternatives, would be more likely to remain in dairying than producers in other provinces.

While the decline, under free trade, of the Canadian dairy industry would be an important development in itself, it is likely that more serious contractions would occur in the secondary industries that use the output of dairy farms as raw materials. Moreover, the dairy-products industry purchases a great deal from other sectors of the Canadian economy,[2] so that a large-scale substitution of imports for domestically produced dairy products may affect the over-all pattern of the Canadian economy.

[1]DBS, *Dairy Statistics*, various issues.
[2]For a discussion of interrelationships in the economy, see T. Josling and G. I. Trant, *Interdependence among Agriculture and Other Sectors of the Canadian Economy*, Agricultural Economics Research Council of Canada, Ottawa.

XI. Poultry and Eggs

Since the Second World War, Canada's poultry industry has been directed primarily towards the domestic market. From 1950 to 1963 poultry exports reached less than 1 percent of total poultry production, while imports were around 3 percent. During the same period Canadian exports of eggs hovered at or below 3 percent, and imports around 1 percent, of production,[1] while virtually all poultry-meat and live-poultry imports into Canada came from the United States.[2] Eggs have been imported from many sources.

There can be little question that changes in production techniques have had a decisive impact on the poultry industry in the last two and a half decades. Within a few years poultry production changed from a small-scale, supplementary, family-owned enterprise, present on nearly every North American farm, to a highly specialized and, by agricultural standards, large-scale enterprise. Before 1945 a typical Canadian chicken flock raised for meat production comprised around five hundred birds; usually only one flock was raised for marketing each year. By 1966 the capacity of a broiler-growing plant in Ontario averaged twenty thousand birds, and at least four lots of birds were produced annually. Turkey and egg production have gone through similar, though less spectacular, expansions.

Poultry production, whether for meat or eggs, has required the following factors of production: baby chicks, feed and medication, housing and fuel, and equipment. All these factors have become so highly developed that a complete poultry plant can be established nearly anywhere. Interchange of production techniques between Canada and the United States has reached an extremely high level. In fact, it would be virtually impossible to tell merely by inspecting the plant whether one was in a Canadian or in a U.S. poultry factory. The essential point is that, although poultry production employs highly specialized techniques, these have become so well developed and widely known that they have become, in a sense, completely mobile across national boundaries.

Canada's competitive position in poultry production vis-à-vis the United States can be compared in the following way. There have been few significant qualitative differences in the resources used for poultry production between the two countries in recent years. However, feed costs have been lower in the United States than in Canada, chiefly because of the U.S. advantage in grain-corn and soybean production. Slightly higher costs are also expected to have prevailed in Canada for poultry equipment (because of Canadian tariffs on these items) and for heating expenditures

[1]Berthiaume, *Exports, Imports, and Domestic Disappearance of Agricultural Products.*
[2]Canada Department of Agriculture, *Canada's Trade in Agricultural Products with the United Kingdom, the United States, and All Countries,* various issues.

(as a consequence of the generally less favourable Canadian climate). Labour costs in Canada have typically been less than in the United States. Furthermore, the poultry industry in the United States has been more highly integrated than in Canada, probably resulting in a slightly higher level of managerial skill.

These differences in factor costs have given U.S. poutry-meat producers a cost advantage over Canadian producers. This advantage is reinforced because feed is a major component of total poultry-meat production costs. Heating and equipment costs tend to raise Canadian production costs, but to a lesser degree. While building costs and labour costs in Canada may have been lower than those in the United States, they represent such a low cost component per bird that they cannot compensate for the higher feed costs in Canada.

Table XXXIII reflects the competitive disadvantage that Canada appears to have in broiler production relative to the United States. Under free trade, Canadian broiler producers would enjoy somewhat lower feed and equipment costs than at present but would still be expected to retain a slight absolute disadvantage relative to the United States.

Relative to poultry-meat production, egg production requires a much larger proportion of labour. The slightly lower cost of Canadian labour relative to U.S. labour can, therefore, more effectively offset the higher Canadian feed prices. This appears to be confirmed by Table XXXIV, which shows that egg prices in Canada have been maintained at lower levels than those in the United States. It may thus be concluded that Canada's egg industry could survive in a satisfactory manner under free trade.

XII. Summary and Conclusions

This survey of Canadian agriculture indicates Canada's strong competitive position vis-à-vis world agriculture. However, Canadian competitiveness appears unevenly distributed among agricultural commodities. Our conclusions have led us to recognize four categories of products, classified by degree of competitiveness:

1. Products in which Canada has a strong absolute advantage:
   wheat, oats, barley, flax, rapeseed, beef feeder cattle, and purebred dairy cattle.
2. Products in which Canada has a slight absolute advantage:
   cheddar cheese and specialty pork products.
3. Products in which Canada has no ascertainable absolute advantage:
   tobacco, grain corn, fresh beef, fresh pork, eggs, soybeans, dried milk powder, and fluid milk.

TABLE XXXIII

CANADIAN AND U.S. DOMESTIC PRICES FOR CHICKEN BROILERS

(cents per pound liveweight in domestic currency)

Year	Country	Jan.	Feb.	Mar.	Apr.	May	June	July	Aug.	Sept.	Oct.	Nov.	Dec.
1961	Canada	17.5	19.0	18.5	16.5	14.5	14.5	16.5	16.5	13.0	12.5	14.5	15.5
	United States	16.4	17.6	16.6	14.9	14.0	12.8	12.4	12.7	11.8	11.8	12.4	15.2
1962	Canada	15.5	16.5	15.5	19.0	17.0	18.0	19.5	20.5	20.5	20.0	14.5	19.0
	United States	16.3	16.7	16.1	14.7	14.3	14.2	15.0	15.5	16.3	15.0	14.1	14.5
1963	Canada	19.0	20.5	19.0	19.5	19.0	18.5	19.0	20.0	20.0	19.0	16.5	19.0
	United States	14.7	15.9	15.5	15.4	14.9	14.4	14.6	14.4	13.9	14.2	14.5	13.3
1964	Canada	18.0	18.5	18.0	16.5	16.5	18.0	20.0	18.0	17.0	17.0	16.5	17.0
	United States	14.2	14.2	14.3	13.7	13.7	14.0	14.8	14.7	14.7	14.4	14.5	13.6
1965	Canada	17.5	19.0	18.5	18.0	17.0	18.5	19.0	19.5	19.5	19.5	19.5	19.5
	United States	14.6	15.1	15.6	15.0	15.4	15.7	15.5	15.2	14.5	14.2	14.6	14.6

Sources: Canadian data: Canada Department of Agriculture, *Poultry Products Market Review*, 1961–65.
U.S. data: U.S. Department of Agriculture, *Supplement to the Poultry and Egg Situation*, revised May 1966.
Note: Canadian prices, given for the Toronto markets, are for broilers and fryers for 1961 and 1962, and for chickens under five pounds from 1963 to 1965.

TABLE XXXIV

EGG PRODUCTION IN CANADA AND CONSUMPTION AND PRICES
IN CANADA AND THE UNITED STATES

	Production	Consumption		Price	
Year	Canada (thousand dozens)	Canada	United States (dozens eggs per capita)	Canada	United States (domestic cents per dozen)
1950	293,727	19.7	30.3	34.9	36.3
1951	291,235	20.0	30.4	48.1	47.7
1952	342,527	22.2	30.2	35.1	41.6
1953	355,184	22.9	29.5	43.0	47.7
1954	385,819	23.9	29.3	33.7	36.6
1955	386,011	24.0	28.8	38.1	39.5
1956	399,758	24.0	28.8	38.1	39.3
1957	439,843	25.0	27.9	31.4	35.9
1958	441,438	24.2	27.3	32.7	38.5
1959	448,236	23.3	26.6	29.2	31.4
1960	435,606	23.0	25.5	29.8	36.0
1961	429,923	22.6	24.7	31.3	35.5
1962	434,200	22.5	24.5	29.9	33.6
1963	417,920	21.5	24.0	33.6	34.4
1964	437,906	21.5	23.6	26.2	33.8
1965	432,795	21.4	23.2	31.4	33.7

Sources: Canadian data: DBS, *Production of Poultry and Eggs*, various issues;
Canada Department of Agriculture, *Poultry Products Market Review*, various issues.
U.S. data: U.S. Department of Agriculture, *Selected Statistical Series for Poultry and Eggs through 1965.*

4. Products in which Canada has an absolute disadvantage:
   fruit and vegetables, sugar, poultry meat, butter, mutton, lamb, and wool.

There can be relatively few surprises in the results presented above. The important grain crops, which account for more than 50 percent of the value of Canada's agricultural exports, show a clear-cut absolute advantage, while relatively few commodities appear to be at an absolute disadvantage. All in all, Canadian agriculture seems to be sufficiently competitive to look after itself in the event of free trade.

Although most of Canadian agriculture buys little from, and sells less to, the rest of the Canadian economy, the beef and the dairy industries provide the essential raw materials for the meat-products industry and the dairy-products industry, respectively. Both these secondary industries contribute substantially to Canadian income by making large purchases from other sectors of the economy. Consequently, the total reduction in Canadian national product resulting from a decline of the Canadian dairy industry under free trade (which may be expected because of Canada's absolute disadvantage in butter production) would be greater than the estimated loss from a contraction of the butter industry alone. Similarly, while Canada appears to have an absolute advantage in feeder-cattle production, increased exports of feeder cattle for fattening and processing in the United States mean a reduction in the output of the meat-products industry. Consequently, the export gain in this case might seem to be illusory in the short run.

Appendix

TABLE A-I

EXPORT CLEARANCES OF CANADIAN WHEAT TO SMALL BUYERS*
INCLUDING COUNTRIES WHICH ARE TRADITIONALLY NET EXPORTERS OF WHEAT
CROP YEARS 1960/61–1964/65

(thousands of bushels)

Destination	1960/61	1961/62	1962/63	1963/64	1964/65
Commonwealth countries:					
Africa:					
Federation of Rhodesia and Nyasaland	109	75	8	37	48
Union of South Africa	—	504	7,883	3,038	945
Asia:					
Hong Kong	524	617	579	668	905
Malaya and Singapore†	—	—	124	453	929
Pakistan	2,099	1,856	362	355	3,199
Caribbean:					
British West Indies	—	—	11	10	12
Europe:					
Malta	1,199	1,238	1,095	1,546	980
Non-Commonwealth countries:					
Africa:					
Mozambique	437	618	562	102	35
Nigeria	—	272	667	651	603
Asia:					
Burma	356	222	—	79	171
Israel	1,592	829	1,789	1,603	529
Kuwait	—	—	—	—	350
Philippines	987	3,855	6,710	7,301	6,482
Saudi Arabia	—	556	648	783	590
Taiwan	140	172	116	411	735
U.S. Oceania	313	474	520	462	76
Europe:					
Albania	2,355	2,102	—	3,696	5,025
Austria	1,529	1,626	1,554	1,191	1,660
Bulgaria	—	—	—	7,586	5,753
Finland	439	2,456	1,682	726	343
France	9,903	1,036	6,877	4,884	5,553
Germany, Eastern	1,918	8,040	—	—	10,552
Ireland	3,413	2,318	3,470	2,235	2,224
Italy	14,933	3,878	4,915	3,875	3,915

TABLE A-I (continued)

Destination	1960/61	1961/62	1962/63	1963/64	1964/65
Norway	3,301	1,729	1,828	1,703	1,601
Sweden	19	30	169	22	67
Switzerland	7,316	8,033	2,923	8,072	3,919
USSR	7,511	—	—	212,204	8,844
Yugoslavia	—	—	3,920	3,502	—
North and Central America:					
Cuba	5	—	—	7,454	8,121
Dominican Republic	923	1,490	1,156	852	704
El Salvador	18	385	580	1,018	777
Guatemala	60	47	255	275	408
Honduras	5	—	—	—	53
Nicaragua	—	—	—	—	505
United States	2,519	1,487	1,169	1,026	—
South America:					
Colombia	—	265	—	—	367
Ecuador	1,191	1,157	1,200	1,087	1,370
Peru	1,816	—	535	731	938
Venezuela	2,658	4,736	6,677	7,904	9,122

Sources: Export clearances for all countries except U.S.: Board of Grain Commissioners for Canada, Statistics Branch, *Canadian Grain Exports*, Ottawa, Queen's Printer, various issues; U.S. data compiled from returns of Canadian elevator licensees and shippers and advice from American grain correspondents.

*Less than 10 million bushels (in latest year shown).

†From 1963/64 on, Malaysia.

TABLE A-II

CUSTOMS EXPORTS OF CANADIAN WHEAT FLOUR TO SMALL BUYERS*
CROP YEARS 1960/61–1964/65
(thousands of bushels)

Destination	1960/61	1961/62	1962/63	1963/64	1964/65
Commonwealth countries:					
Africa:					
Gambia	—	—	—	8	63
Nigeria	852	1,752	550	18	8
Federation of Rhodesia and Nyasaland	38	33	38	31	2
Asia:					
Aden	—	—	—	—	28
British Middle East	15	32	28	38	20
Europe:					
Gibraltar	31	64	36	32	3
Caribbean:					
British Honduras	18	36	37	40	43
Oceania:					
Fiji	7	6	4	6	8
South America:					
British Guiana (Guyana)	203	31	23	39	57

TABLE A-II continued

Destination	1960/61	1961/62	1962/63	1963/64	1964/65
Non-Commonwealth countries:					
Africa:					
Angola	18	—	4	6	7
Cameroon Republic	—	—	—	—	48
French Equatorial Africa	5	4	—	—	25
Guinea Republic	—	—	—	—	1
Ivory Coast	—	—	—	3	4
Liberia	19	36	65	61	85
Malawi	—	—	—	—	21
Mozambique	5	21	27	34	43
Nyasaland	—	—	—	—	11
Tanganyika†	17	33	15	11	2
Asia:					
Indonesia	206	390	153	126	17
Iran	2	2	4	4	2
Japan	1,588	1,081	516	85	47
Jordan	1	110	1	1	10
Kuwait	26	25	77	31	10
Portuguese Asia	44	16	10	21	14
Saudi Arabia	9	1	7	6	1
Syria	7	2	6	1	1
Europe:					
Denmark	2	3	11	5	3
Greece	10	7	30	16	16
Iceland	17	24	15	5	3
Italy	4	19	5	1	7
Netherlands	6	2	5	6	8
North and Central America:					
El Salvador	190	215	83	12	2
French West Indies	4	2	4	2	8
Guatemala	62	81	52	16	46
Haiti	—	—	28	110	22
Honduras	76	105	68	64	50
Nicaragua	381	463	489	277	2
Panama	324	440	419	155	80
St. Pierre and Miquelon	7	10	16	21	21
South America:					
Chile	12	8	12	6	1
Peru	5	22	41	64	75
Surinam	83	76	67	74	80
Venezuela	35	11	2	—	1
Oceania:					
French Oceania	1	1	2	1	1
U.S. Oceania	29	2	3	2	14

Source: Canadian Wheat Board, *Annual Report*, various issues.
*Less than 100,000 bushels (in latest year shown).
†From 1964/65 on, Tanzania.

BARLEY PRODUCTION AND PRICES, ANNUALLY, 1948-65

| | Canada | | | | | United States | | | |
| | Production | | | Average farm price* | | Production | | | Average price*§ ($/bu.) |
Crop year	Total acres seeded (000 acres)	Total yield (mil. bu.)	Average yield per seeded acre (bu.)	Canada ($/bu.)	Ontario ($/bu.)	Total acres seeded† (mil. acres)	Total yield (mil. bu.)	Average yield per seeded acre‡ (bu.)	
1948	6.4	152.3	23.8	0.96	1.11	13.1	315.5	24.2	1.16
1949	5.9	118.0	19.9	1.31	1.25	11.1	237.1	21.3	1.06
1950	6.5	167.5	25.7	1.13	1.30	13.0	303.8	23.3	1.19
1951	7.8	245.4	31.3	1.10	1.30	10.8	257.2	23.8	1.26
1952	8.5	291.6	34.4	1.06	1.35	9.2	228.2	24.8	1.37
1953	8.9	262.1	29.4	0.86	1.07	9.6	246.7	25.7	1.17
1954	7.8	175.2	22.3	0.89	1.06	14.7	379.3	25.7	1.09
1955	9.9	251.1	25.4	0.87	1.05	16.3	403.1	24.7	0.92
1956	8.4	269.1	32.1	0.79	1.06	14.7	376.7	25.6	0.99
1957	9.4	216.0	23.0	0.76	0.98	16.4	442.8	27.0	0.887
1958	9.3	237.8	25.6	0.77	0.98	16.2	477.4	29.6	0.90
1959	7.7	215.6	27.3	0.74	0.99	16.8	422.4	25.1	0.86
1960	6.9	193.5	28.2	0.80	0.99	15.6	431.3	27.6	0.838
1961	5.5	112.6	20.4	1.05	1.05	15.8	395.7	25.1	0.981
1962	5.3	165.9	31.4		1.068	14.7	429.5	29.2	0.927
1963	6.2	220.7	35.8		1.078	11.6	405.6	35.1	
1964	5.5	166.8	30.6		1.078	1.1	403.1	37.8	
1965‖	6.0	214.6	35.5			9.5	207.7	42.8	

Sources: Canadian data: DBS, *Handbook of Agricultural Statistics, 1908–63*, and Ontario Department of Agriculture, *Agricultural Statistics for Ontario*, 1964; supplementary data received through direct communication with DBS. U.S. data: U.S. Department of Agriculture, *Agricultural Statistics*, various issues.

*All prices in domestic currencies.

†Estimates of seeded average relate to the over-all average of barley sown for all purposes, including barley sown in the preceding fall.

‡Calculated from total acres seeded and total yield.

§Obtained by weighting state prices by quantity sold. Includes an allowance for loans redeemed at the end of the crop marketing season and for quantities bought by the government under purchase agreements when such transactions are of significant volume.

‖Preliminary for Canada.

TABLE A-IV

OAT PRODUCTION AND PRICES, ANNUALLY, 1948–65

Crop year	Canada Production			Average farm price		United States Production			Average price‡ ($/bu.)
	Total acres seeded (000 acres)	Total yield (mil. bu.)	Average yield per seeded acre (bu.)	Canada ($/bu.)	Ontario ($/bu.)	Total acres seeded* (mil. acres)	Total yield (mil. bu.)	Average yield per seeded acre† (bu.)	
1948	10.8	345.3	31.8	0.70	0.82	43.8	1,450	33.1	0.717
1949	11.0	304.6	27.7	0.79	0.84	43.1	1,220	28.3	0.655
1950	11.2	401.8	35.9	0.78	0.90	45.0	1,369	30.4	0.788
1951	11.9	493.9	41.5	0.76	0.89	41.0	1,278	31.2	0.820
1952	11.1	471.1	42.6	0.67	0.82	42.3	1,217	28.8	0.789
1953	9.9	414.0	41.9	0.63	0.72	43.2	1,153	26.7	0.742
1954	10.0	306.4	30.5	0.67	0.77	46.9	1,410	30.1	0.714
1955	11.0	399.4	36.5	0.67	0.76	47.5	1,496	31.5	0.600
1956	10.5	467.5	44.6	0.58	0.78	44.2	1,151	26.0	0.686
1957	8.8	316.9	35.9	0.61	0.70	41.8	1,290	30.8	0.605
1958	9.2	345.7	37.4	0.64	0.71	37.7	1,401	37.2	0.578
1959	9.1	344.2	37.9	0.69	0.74	35.1	1,052	30.0	0.646
1960	9.6	398.5	41.4	0.68	0.76	31.5	1,155	36.6	0.598
1961	8.5	284.0	33.2	0.75	0.81	32.5	1,011	31.1	0.641
1962§	10.6	493.6	46.6		0.80	30.2	1,032	34.2	0.617
1963	9.5	453.1	47.8		0.776				
1964	8.2	357.2	43.6		0.771				
1965‖	8.7	415.0	47.9						

Sources: Canadian data: 1962–64 Ontario prices from Ontario Department of Agriculture, *Agricultural Statistics for Ontario, 1964*; all other Canadian data from DBS, *Handbook of Agricultural Statistics, 1908–63* (also data by province, brought up to date from DBS data).

U.S. data: 1948 data from U.S. Department of Agriculture, *Agricultural Statistics 1962*; 1949–62 data from *Agricultural Statistics, 1963*.

*Estimates of seeded average relate to the total average of oats sown for all purposes, including oats sown in the preceding fall.

†Calculated from data of seeded acres and production.

‡Obtained by weighting state prices by quantity sold. Includes an allowance for loans unredeemed at the end of the crop marketing season and for quantities bought by the government under purchase agreements when such transactions are of significant volume.

TABLE A-V

TOBACCO PRODUCTION AND PRICES—ALL TYPES OF TOBACCO, ANNUALLY, 1948-64

Crop year	Total acres harvested (000 acres) Canada	Total acres harvested (000 acres) Ontario	Production (mil. lbs.) Canada	Production (mil. lbs.) Ontario	Average farm price (¢ per lb.) Canada	Average farm price (¢ per lb.) Ontario	United States Total acres harvested (000 acres)	United States Production* (mil. lbs.)	United States Average yield per acre harvested (lbs.)	United States Average price per lb. received by farmer (¢)
1948	111	98	127	113	39.7	41.01	1,554	1,980	1,274	48.2
1949	109	99	140	132	39.7	40.57	1,623	1,969	1,213	45.9
1950	102	93	120	111	42.64	43.85	1,599	2,030	1,269	51.7
1951	119	110	154	145	43.05	45.83	1,780	2,332	1,310	51.1
1952	92	84	140	131	40.74	41.20	1,772	2,256	1,273	49.9
1953	101	92	139	129	42.82	43.57	1,633	2,059	1,261	52.3
1954	132	121	185	174	42.10	42.73	1,667	2,244	1,346	51.1
1955	110	97	135	121	42.78	44.25	1,495	2,193	1,466	53.2
1956	128	116	162	152	44.50	45.52	1,363	2,176	1,596	53.7
1957	137	127	165	156	47.67	48.38	1,122	1,667	1,486	56.1
1958	134	125	197	188	45.4	45.83	1,078	1,736	1,611	59.9
1959	128	118	170	158	53.2	54.18	1,153	1,796	1,558	58.3
1960	136	124	214	200	53.56	54.58	1,142	1,944	1,703	60.9
1961	138	127	210	198	50.23	51.13	1,174	2,061	1,755	63.8
1962†	131	122	203	190	47.24	50.50	1,226	2,309	1,884	59.0
1963	114	104	201	190	45.06	45.48				
1964	85	76	154	143	54.08	54.81				

Sources: Canadian data: DBS, *Reference Papers*, 1950, *Canada Year Book*, 1949, *Leaf Tobacco Acreage, Production, and Value, Quarterly Bulletin of Agricultural Statistics*.

U.S. data: 1948 data from U.S. Department of Agriculture, *Agricultural Statistics*, 1962; 1949–62 data from *Agricultural Statistics*, 1963.

*Production figures are on a farm-sales-weight basis.

†Preliminary for United States.

TABLE A-VI

FLUE-CURED TOBACCO PRODUCTION AND PRICES, ANNUALLY, 1948–64

	Canada						United States			
	Total acres harvested ('000 acres)		Production				Production			
			Total yield (mil. lbs.)		Average farm price (¢ per lb.)				Average yield per acre harvested (lbs.)	Average price per lb. received by farmer (¢)
Crop year	Canada	Ontario	Canada	Ontario	Canada	Ontario	Total acres harvested ('000 acres)	Total yield* (mil. lbs.)		
1948	91	85	102	98	42.5	42.7				
1949	91	86	117	114	42.1	42.25	935	1,114	1,191	47.2
1950	92	87	108	104	44.49	44.72	958	1,257	1,312	54.7
1951	111	106	144	140	44.24	46.44	1,110	1,453	1,309	52.4
1952	86	81	132	127	41.73	41.61	1,111	1,365	1,229	50.3
1953	96	91	132	127	43.70	43.77	1,022	1,272	1,245	52.8
1954	123	117	173	168	43.18	43.21	1,042	1,314	1,261	52.7
1955	98	92	118	112	45.29	45.48	991	1,483	1,479	52.7
1956	118	111	149	144	46.11	46.30	875	1,422	1,625	51.5
1957	126	121	152	148	49.23	49.29	663	975	1,471	55.4
1958	123	117	181	176	46.54	46.57	639	1,081	1,691	58.2
1959	117	111	152	147	55.39	55.57	693	1,081	1,559	58.3
1960	129	124	205	199	54.55	54.65	692	1,251	1,808	60.4
1961	128	122	195	190	51.58	51.70	698	1,258	1,801	64.3
1962†	122	117	188	180	48.28	51.04	731	1,400	1,916	60.1
1963	106	99	187	180	45.92	45.81				
1964	80	73	143	137	55.61	55.63				

Sources: Canadian data: DBS, *Reference Papers*, 1950, *Canada Year Book*, 1949, *Leaf Tobacco Acreage, Production, and Value, Quarterly Bulletin of Agricultural Statistics.*
U.S. data: 1949–57 data from U.S. Department of Agriculture, *Agricultural Statistics*, 1962; 1958 from *Agricultural Statistics*, 1963.
Note: Premiums for farm-typing and grading of flue-cured tobacco have not been applicable beginning with the 1958 crop (except in Ontario).
*Production figures are on a farm-sales-weight basis.
†Preliminary for United States.

TABLE A-VII

EXPORTS OF UNMANUFACTURED TOBACCO
SELECTED YEARS
(metric tons)

Exporting region*	1948–52	1958	1963
Europe	108,000	162,000	193,000
EEC	11,000	19,600	20,000
Bulgaria	44,600	43,800	86,000
Czechoslovakia	—	1,900	3,000
Greece	28,900	62,400	62,000
Hungary	7,600	—	—
Poland	—	1,500	3,000
United Kingdom†	4,600	1,100	1,500
Yugoslavia	10,600	23,200	17,000
North and Central America	255,000	270,000	263,000
Canada	11,500	13,400	17,800
Cuba	14,400	26,000	—
Dominican Republic	16,100	11,500	—
Honduras	1,900	—	1,500
Mexico	200	300	12,500
United States‡	210,400	218,800	230,800
South America	38,000	39,000	83,600
Argentina	400	1,700	17,500
Brazil	29,600	30,400	44,300
Colombia	3,800	4,500	11,200
Paraguay	3,900	2,400	10,600
Asia	127,000	210,000	154,000
China, Taiwan	—	200	1,300
Cyprus	600	800	1,000
India	42,400	48,100	67,900
Japan	400	3,700	6,900
Philippines	6,000	14,100	24,800
Syria (UAR)‡	1,900	300	1,500
Thailand	—	5,800	3,800
Turkey	58,600	56,100	44,600
Africa	69,000	81,000	104,300
Algeria	11,200	7,800	—
Cameroon	400	1,000	1,000
Madagascar	3,100	4,300	3,700
Rhodesia, Nyasaland†	1,800	65,000	96,800
USSR	—	6,200	1,800

Source: FAO, *Trade Yearbook*, various issues.

*Countries exporting 1,000 metric tons or more in 1963.

†Including re-exports.

‡From September 28, 1961, on, Syria.

TABLE A-VIII

IMPORTS OF UNMANUFACTURED TOBACCO
SELECTED YEARS
(metric tons)

Importing region*	1948/52	1958	1963
Europe	350,000	464,000	584,700
EEC	125,600	177,000	263,600
EFTA	178,000	194,000	209,900
Czechoslovakia	—	15,500	13,000
Finland	4,500	4,800	7,000
Germany, Democratic Republic†	—	18,900	29,200
Ireland	8,100	6,100	6,400
Poland	4,800	11,800	19,300
Spain	21,100	29,300	26,900
Yugoslavia	1,200	900	10,000
North and Central America	47,000	71,000	84,900
Canada	800	1,300	1,200
El Salvador	1,200	1,500	1,400
Mexico	1,000	2,400	2,600
United States	42,600	62,900	76,100
South America	10,000	3,000	5,600
Argentina	4,700	—	—
Chile	300	300	2,100
Uruguay	3,600	1,700	2,700
Asia	46,000	56,000	41,200
Ceylon	700	600	1,200
China, Taiwan	100	500	2,200
Hong Kong	5,200	5,000	8,300
Israel	600	800	1,500
Japan	2,500	2,700	15,800
Philippines	6,600	2,400	2,300
Thailand	1,700	5,300	3,700
Vietnam, Republic of	—	1,800	2,500
Africa	37,000	40,000	32,900
Congo, Leopoldville	—	—	4,000
Morocco	4,000	2,600	4,000
Nigeria	2,500	2,400	1,700
South Africa	1,800	1,400	2,400
Tunisia	2,800	3,700	2,200
United Arab Republic	12,500	11,900	12,400
Oceania	15,000	23,000	15,500
Australia	12,200	19,400	12,400
New Zealand	2,700	3,400	2,500
USSR	—	84,300	93,400

Source: FAO, *Trade Yearbook*, various issues.

*Countries importing 1,000 metric tons or more in 1963.

†Data are estimates based on import and export data by origin or destination of countries reporting trade, or were derived from unofficial sources by the FAO.

Prospects
for Trade Liberalization In Agriculture

David L. MacFarlane and Lewis A. Fischer

I. Introduction

The problem

The agricultural industries of the North Atlantic area are characterized by a jungle of laws and regulations aimed largely at raising the level of prices and the incomes of farmers. The jungle consists of tariffs, national price supports and production-control programs, import-quota arrangements, European Common Market negotiations for a Common Agricultural Policy (CAP), export subsidies and provision of credit for surplus disposal, state trading, and international commodity agreements. These policy measures, taken at a national level or at the level of a regional trading bloc such as the EEC, have led to severe restrictions on international trade in farm products. In fact, throughout the history of postwar trade negotiations, agriculture has been given "special status," meaning that it has been practically exempt from such negotiations. In view of all these circumstances, the economist can with only limited profit employ customary analytical procedures.[1]

There are two challenges to the writers of this study. The first, related to the task of evaluating the prospects for trade liberalization in agriculture, is to cut through the maze of political factors that afflict the industry. Only

[1]While agricultural trade restrictions in all their varied forms have become noticeably worse during the post-1945 period, their historical roots go back a very long way. By 1800 most European countries and Britain had well-developed mechanisms for protecting their domestic farm industries. Then Britain began in 1844 a period of some ninety years of free trade, and the consequences were what the economists would expect: lower land rents and farm-labour returns. These were accompanied by extreme hardship in the farm areas. While the major countries which developed as agricultural exporters in the nineteenth century maintained and encouraged a climate of economic freedom for the agricultural sectors, this came to an end with the depression of the 1930s. From that time until the present, importing and exporting countries have appeared to vie with one another in devising measures for the protection of their agriculture. As we shall see, there are indications that, in the 1960s, this climate has been changing. There is a good prospect that serious discussion of the costs of agricultural protectionism and of the possible gains from freeing the farm industry will be possible.

in this way can we determine whether (and in what forms) freer trade in farm products might be realized. An equally difficult task is to assess the effects of such possible changes on agricultural trade patterns, on farm output, on the prices of farm products, and on the incomes of farmers.

Stated in other terms, the purpose of this study is to assess whether an accommodation can be negotiated between the apparent need for agricultural supports and the desirability of maintaining and expanding trade in farm products. In doing this, we must keep in mind that the intricate network of controls that now distinguishes agriculture arose in large part from two special characteristics of the industry. Historically, both in countries that employ widespread use of restrictive measures and in those that do not, labour returns have been much lower in agriculture than in other industries. In addition, farm prices and incomes are subject to highly erratic fluctuations, in part associated with irregular yields and output, leading to a high degree of instability in the industry.

The difficulty of breaking through the maze of controls must not be underestimated. National governments have shown a willingness to discuss their problems on an international level but have shown little interest in reform at home. Nevertheless, there are some signs that encourage us to make this analysis of the opportunities for trade liberalization. Recognition of the costs, both to the importing and to the exporting countries, of the ludicrous policies employed over the past two decades may now be leading to more rational farm and trade policies. In the past four years there has been a clear improvement in farm prices and incomes, and in the United States this has been accompanied by the freeing of one farm product after another from some of the most objectionable controls.

Scope and method

The development of an Atlantic trading community is a particularly interesting approach to the freeing of agriculture from international trade and other restrictions. For present purposes an Atlantic trading group would include Canada, the United States, the European Economic Community (EEC), the European Free Trade Association (EFTA), and possibly the Caribbean countries not already members of the Latin American Free Trade Area (LAFTA).

Although emphasis is placed on the Atlantic grouping, prospective trade with Japan, the USSR, eastern Europe, and China, and with the developing countries will greatly influence trends in the Atlantic community and must be taken into account. The other explicit assumptions underlying this study are as follows. (1) There will be no change in foreign exchange rates. (2) Since non-tariff barriers are inordinately important in agriculture, it is assumed that progress in reducing them must accompany, and be harmonized with, reductions in tariff barriers. (3) Since it is highly unrealistic in the case of agriculture to suggest, even for purposes of economic analysis, either a rapid or a total removal of barriers, it is assumed that there will be a gradual removal of both. Implicit in this assumption is the continuance by governments of some protective or stabilizing measures to aid their farm industries. In this context, a transition period of five to twenty years is suggested. (4) An overriding assumption is that the long-term objective of international trade policy is the most rapid sustainable growth of the world economy as a whole.

The study will consider, first, the postwar agricultural trade patterns (particularly in the North Atlantic community) applicable to those Canadian farm products that are important in foreign trade. It will then turn to an examination of the maze of national, regional, and international policies that influence Canada's present and prospective trading position in agriculture vis-à-vis that of important competitors. This will be followed by a consideration of the prospects for freer trade in farm products in the North Atlantic area and of the means by which this might be realized, taking account of the nature of the barriers. And finally, the implications of freer trade for Canadian farm producers will be considered.

II. The Canadian Farm Industry and Its Foreign Trade

The Canadian farm industry accounts for about 4 to 6 percent of net national product.[1] Annual gross output of the industry ranged, during the period 1950–65, from a low of $2,122 million in 1950 to a high of $3,776 million in 1965. During the same period, annual net output ranged from a low of $975 million in 1961 to a high of $1,645 million in 1965.

Canada is the world's fourth largest exporter of farm products. These exports represent about one-third of Canadian farm production. Total Canadian agricultural exports increased substantially between the early 1950s and 1963–64, when they averaged $1,530 million. In the early postwar years, farm exports accounted for between one-quarter and one-third of Canada's total merchandise exports; in recent years they have accounted for about 20 percent.

Trends in Canada's agricultural trade

Some interesting changes have taken place in the destination of Canadian farm exports. Until the early 1950s, the United States was Canada's most

[1]Moreover, by their non-farm work, members of the agricultural labour force make an additional contribution estimated at half their contribution through agriculture.

TABLE I

CANADA, MAJOR AGRICULTURAL EXPORTS, BY COMMODITY, 1956 AND 1961–65
(thousands of dollars)

Commodity	1956	1961	1962	1963	1964	1965
Total exports	4,789,746	5,754,985	6,178,631	6,798,500	8,094,360	8,522,953
Agricultural products	959,741	1,223,584	1,187,949	1,275,040	1,624,605	1,525,920
as percentage of all products	20.0	21.3	19.2	18.7	20.1	17.9
Wheat and wheat flour	584,630	724,267	658,561	849,420	1,123,771	906,580
Barley	94,977	48,966	29,927	24,524	51,254	43,679
Other cereals—milled and unmilled	32,759	30,605	30,567	40,613	33,646	35,432
Flaxseed	43,623	46,269	41,920	38,560	48,662	51,658
Rapeseed	3,000	13,850	20,667	16,156	10,152	30,900
Oil seed—cake and meal	20,891	11,419	19,064	23,123	22,409	26,485
Other feeds of vegetable origin	8,563	10,750	12,977	19,007	22,082	21,276
Vegetables and vegetable preparations	8,851	15,810	23,998	27,341	30,943	41,889
Other crude vegetable products	11,485	13,227	13,856	12,512	13,233	14,053
Fruits and fruit preparations	11,791	13,226	17,691	22,768	21,636	20,093
Tobacco	17,674	28,025	35,182	29,541	38,365	35,363
Live animals	12,948	66,901	68,054	41,971	34,514	79,133
Meats and meat preparations	37,035	42,898	42,781	44,421	51,698	76,244
Other animal products	24,056	20,593	20,785	19,637	21,496	33,539

Source: Dominion Bureau of Statistics, *Trade of Canada, Exports,* and *Canada Yearbook,* various years.

important customer, taking almost half our total farm exports. With the institution in the 1950s of U.S. quantitative import restrictions arising from their farm programs, this market has been effectively eroded, so that in 1963–64 it accounted for only 14 percent of agricultural exports. The USSR, eastern European countries, and mainland China have become important importers of wheat and accounted for 25 percent of total farm exports in 1963–64. The EEC countries reduced their shares from over 16 percent in the period 1954–58 to 12 percent in 1963–64. On the other hand, other countries increased their shares from 14 percent in 1950–51 to 19 percent in 1963–64. Japan's remained relatively constant in the decade from 1954–64.

If wheat is excluded from agricultural exports, a somewhat different picture emerges. Prior to 1939, over 60 percent of Canada's agricultural exports (excluding wheat) found markets in Britain, and one-quarter in the United States. In recent years the situation has reversed, with only 25 percent of these products going to Britain, and nearly one-half to the United States.[2] EEC countries take about 10 percent, followed by Japan with a somewhat smaller share.

Wheat and wheat flour are by far the most important among Canadian farm exports, in terms of both the value of exports and the proportion of production sold abroad. In the 1960s, average annual exports have been 435 million bushels, valued at about $853 million. These two commodities have accounted for some 60 percent of agricultural exports since 1960. Among the other grains, only barley exports have been on a scale sufficient to warrant mention here. These have averaged 38 million bushels annually, valued at about $40 million in the crop years of the 1960s. All other cereals, processed and unprocessed, have had export values of about $35 million annually.

Other crop exports worthy of note are the oilseeds (flaxseed and rapeseed): annual exports of flaxseed have averaged about $45 million annually, and those of rapeseed about $18 million. Tobacco exports have been averaging about $30 million. There have been relatively small exports of fruits and vegetables and processed preparations from them, such as maple products, seeds, and fodder.

In the category of livestock and livestock products, exports of live animals, particularly feeder cattle, slaughter cattle, and dairy cattle, have been most important, averaging about $58 million annually in the 1960s. Other animal products (hides and skins, other meats and meat preparations) have averaged about $70 million annually. Cheese exports, largely

2F. S. Shefrin, *Trends in Canada's Agricultural Trade Pattern*, Ottawa, Department of Agriculture, 1966, p. 9.

to Britain under an export subsidy scheme, have averaged about 25 million pounds a year, valued at some $10 million.

In the Atlantic area, Britain has been the largest buyer of Canadian wheat, averaging over 70 million bushels a year. EEC countries have been purchasing 60 to 70 million bushels annually. Purchases by Japan have been averaging about 50 million bushels a year. Eastern European countries and the USSR have made large purchases in recent years, as has mainland China. However, the prospect is that most of these countries will again become self-sufficient in a relatively short period. South American and Caribbean countries have been purchasing 20 to 25 million bushels annually in recent years. A minuscule import quota is applicable to Canadian wheat exports to the United States.

The destination of Canadian barley exports is largely the Common Market countries, Britain, Japan, the United States, and China. Oilseed exports go mainly to Britain, the Common Market countries, and Japan. Tobacco is exported very largely to Britain under a preferential tariff arrangement.

Virtually all live animals and fresh, chilled, and frozen meats are exported to the United States. Other meats and meat products are also exported mainly to the United States, as well as to the EEC countries and Britain. Hides and skins, offal products, and tallow are shipped largely to the United States, the Common Market countries, and to Britain. As we have noted, almost all Canadian cheese exports go to Britain.

Canada has very large food imports. In 1963–64, they averaged $1,022 million, compared with agricultural exports averaging $1,530 million. A fairly large proportion (perhaps one-third) are imports of products which are produced in Canada, and this proportion has been increasing over the past ten years. Canada has sizable imports of feed grains, of temperate-climate fruits and vegetables, and of meats, as well as of poultry and dairy products. The increased imports of some of these products suggest Canadian agriculture has not made technological (and cost) progress comparable to that of the United States, from which a very large proportion of these imports come. Most of the food imports from the United States are processed, and their import into Canada reflects the existence of larger-scale and more-efficient processing plants in the United States.

Canada's position in world trade in farm products

Since a separate study in the present series is devoted to Canada's comparative-cost or comparative-advantage position, only a few summary points will be made here. In the study referred to, Professor Gerald I. Trant[3] has grouped farm products according to their competitive position. According to his grouping, products in which Canada has a strong absolute advantage are wheat, oats, barley, flax, rapeseed, beef feeder cattle, and pure-bred dairy cattle. Products in which Canada has a slight absolute advantage include cheddar cheese and specialty pork products. Products in which Canada has no ascertainable absolute advantage are tobacco, grain corn, fresh beef, fresh pork, eggs, soybeans, dried milk powder, and fluid milk. Products in which Canada has an absolute disadvantage include fruits and vegetables, sugar, poultry meat, butter, mutton, lamb, and wool.

Dr. G. A. MacEachern states about Canada that "a relatively stable absolute advantage is enjoyed by many commodities, for example, wheat, barley, flaxseed, rapeseed, milk production, grade dairy cattle, some cheeses, and other milk products, tobacco, turnips, and some fruit. For a number of other commodities, a competitive advantage exists with selected countries, but is unstable relative to the United States, varying by seasons of the year and due to regional production and transport costs, for example, feeder and slaughter cattle, hogs, a variety of meats, eggs, apples, and potatoes."[4]

There is substantial agreement between these two writers in regard to Canada's comparative advantage in farm products.

III. The Atlantic Area Farm-Policy Maze

The prospects for greater Canadian trade in farm products in the Atlantic region depend on three factors: (1) the demand for farm products in the area, (2) the degree of competitive advantage (in a purely economic context) which Canada enjoys, and (3) the adjustment of the complex of barriers that now inhibit trade. The first and third of these are examined in some detail in the following pages, with emphasis placed on Canada's position and the effects of freer trade on Canadian agriculture. The second has just been touched on here, it being the subject of a separate study in this series.

Trade liberalization possibilities cannot be explored without first examin-

[3]"The Impact of Trade Liberalization on Canadian Agriculture," in the present volume.
[4]G. A. MacEachern and David L. MacFarlane, "The Relative Position of Canadian Agriculture in World Trade," *Conference on International Trade and Canadian Agriculture*, Economic Council of Canada and the Agricultural Economics Research Council of Canada, Ottawa, Queen's Printer, 1966, p. 134.

ing the agricultural policies of the major trading countries and blocs in the Atlantic area. Of particular importance are those policy aspects that have resulted in barriers to trade in agricultural products.

One of the most significant economic phenomena of the postwar years has been the agricultural protectionist measures adopted by most countries in the world. Incomes of agricultural workers in the more developed countries have been one-third to two-thirds lower than those earned by comparable workers in the non-agricultural sectors of the various economies. Virtually all governments around the world have developed domestic programs to assist agriculture, partly as a result of political pressure from farm people, and to some extent in the hope that agricultural aids would speed the rationalization of the industry. But the success of these programs has required the increased use of barriers to agricultural imports.

The European Economic Community

The most significant developments in agricultural policy of the past decade and a half, and certainly within the context of this study, are those of the European Economic Community. Over a protracted period of discussion and negotiation, these countries maintained the policy of increasingly protecting their farmers. In fact, failure to agree on the Common Agricultural Policy (CAP) continually threatened the disintegration of the Community. Only in late 1966, after a year's boycott of negotiations by France on the issue of supranationality, was the CAP agreed upon. It became effective on July 1, 1968.

The basis of agreement is the creation of a common internal agricultural market (with a few temporary exceptions in cases of special difficulty) and of a system of import levies aimed at bringing import prices of basic commodities to the level of those established by the EEC Commission. Provisions have been made for fixed tariffs on some products and for quantitative restrictions of imports if they should threaten the farmers of any signatory country. The levies will be paid into the European Agricultural Guidance and Guarantee Fund. Member countries have been paying assessments into the Fund since 1962 and will continue to do so until the CAP is fully operative. In the first year, assessments totalled $36.2 million (U.S.) and were expected to rise to $700 million in 1966–67. It is expected that the levies will yield to the Fund more than $1,500 million in the first year of its operation.

The Fund will be used for three purposes: (1) price supports and export subsidies, (2) measures designed to improve the structure of agriculture, and (3) special payments to Germany, Italy, and Luxembourg to compensate for the reduction of grain prices in these countries. Estimates are that 65 percent of the sum will be used for the first purpose, 21 percent for the second, and 14 percent for the third.

Dr. J. A. Richter[1] writes of the CAP arrangements:

To sum up the main content of the EEC's agricultural market and price policy, we might say that the most rigid protection is planned for the basic (so-called target price) commodities. Others will be more flexibly protected. Grains, sugar, and dairy products are the basic commodities for which target prices are to be approximated systematically by variable import levies and/or subsidies.

Pork, eggs, and poultry will be protected by fixed tariffs and 'derived' variable levies. . . . Fruits and vegetables will be mainly protected by fixed tariffs and market interventions.

For products other than the basic ones . . . , minimum import or gate prices may be decreed and realized by special levies.

For oilseeds, it is not unlikely that a system of manufacturing taxes (margarine) will be imposed to regulate interproduct competition affecting highly protected animal fats.

Of greatest interest to Canada is the protection afforded wheat producers within the Community. In recent years about one-third of the gross wheat imports into the EEC were supplied by Canada. The threshold price of wheat (the price applicable to imports at the frontier which would assure that the internal target price, and thus the farm price, would be guaranteed) was set in 1964 at $3.12 (Can.). The difference between the landed price at the frontier and the threshold price is covered by a variable levy.

While the CAP provides guidelines for agricultural development in each of the member countries, each member country will continue to pursue its own internal policies with respect to agriculture, to the extent that they do not interfere with the provisions of the CAP. It is very difficult to secure complete and reliable data concerning the costs of the purely internal programs, but it has been estimated that they currently cost over $2 billion (U.S.) and will rise to $2.5 billion by 1970. Thus, through the internal domestic programs and the levies, the total cost of farm programs will probably exceed $4 billion in 1970. This should be considered in the context of a projected GNP for the Community of $280 billion (U.S.) in that year. An additional burden is created by the fact that food prices in the Community are inordinately high.

In addition to the maintenance of a wide measure of independence in agricultural policy in individual Common Market countries, these countries also have widely differing agricultural-resource endowments. Before assessing the implications for Canada of the CAP, we will examine the farm industries within the Community—first in France, which is by far the

[1]*Agricultural Protection and Trade: Proposals for an International Policy*, New York, Praeger, 1964, pp. 33–4.

largest agricultural producer (and a surplus producer interested in markets now shared by Canada), and then in the other five countries, which are important customers for our commercial agricultural exports.

France joined the EEC partly because she believed she would become the breadbasket of, and a dominant supplier of other farm products to, the Community. Forty-six percent of the Community's farm land is in France. When the French government stated that in 1963–64 there were ten million acres of uncultivated farm land, it created the myth of the gigantic potential of French agriculture. While there are significant possibilities of augmenting aggregate farm output by employing presently unused land, these possibilities are questionable, at least for the near future.

Of the 86 million acres of farm land currently in use in France, some 35 million require consolidation. The Fourth Plan foresees the consolidation of 1.7 million acres per year at a cost of $60 million per year of public funds. In other words, twenty, if not twenty-five, years would be needed to implement this project.[2]

Land devoted to the nine leading crops decreased 15 percent, from 13 million hectares to 11 million hectares, from the beginning of the 1950s to 1962–63. Nonetheless, acreage of wheat, corn, and barley increased over these years. The farm-labour force decreased at an annual rate of 3 to 4 percent, but this was accompanied by an increase in farm output averaging 4.2 percent per year. Purchased inputs, such as fertilizers and farm machinery, account for much of the production increases over the period. Table II shows striking increases of these inputs in the 1950s. Tractors have increased over the twelve-year period to more than five times their initial number.

In the early 1960s about 150,000 persons of African origin were employed in French agriculture. The majority will leave the country soon under present French policies. Their replacement suggests the substitution of more-expensive labour and/or further mechanization.

State aids to agriculture were $400 million (U.S.) in 1954, $733 million in 1959, $1,322 million in 1962, and $1,763 million in 1964–65. More than one-half of the last figure was used as an aid to the production adjustments. Income supports ranked next, followed by export subsidies. Farmers' terms of trade have improved markedly, since prices received by farmers increased by 22 percent during the period 1960 to 1964, while the prices paid by farmers rose by only 8 percent over the same period.

The choice of the commodities selected for support takes account of preferential status implied in membership in the EEC, as well as of the

---

[2]Ambassade de France, *France and Agriculture*, New York, Service de Presse et d'Information, p. 8. Unless otherwise indicated, data are from this publication.

TABLE II

FRANCE, SELECTED PURCHASED INPUTS IN AGRICULTURE

Input	1948-49 to 1952-53	1962-63	1962-63 inputs as percent of 1948-49 to 1952-53 inputs
Fertilizers ('000 metric tons)			
Nitrogenous	252	683	171
Phosphate	454	1,034	128
Potash	362	910	151
Tractors	148,142	804,400	443
Combined harvester-threshers	17,738	68,500	286

Source: United Nations, Food and Agriculture Organization, *Production Yearbook*, no. 18, Rome, 1964.

TABLE III

FRANCE, AIDS TO AGRICULTURE, 1964-65

Type of Aid	Amount (mil. $ U.S.)
Export subsidies	237.5
Income support	513.8
Aids to adjustment of production	890.7
Other	121.0
Total	1,763.0

Source: *Agrarpolitische Revue*, Brugg, Switzerland, April 1965, p. 306.

shifting demand resulting from improved incomes in western Europe. Another factor in French policy is the planned expansion of trade with both underdeveloped and eastern European countries.

In summary, the main objectives of current French agricultural policy are to control the grain market in West Germany and Benelux by displacing wheat imports from non-members, particularly the United States, and to expand animal production in order to benefit from the increasing demand for meat throughout the EEC. There are no limits on meat production in the current French plan.

The value of final agricultural production increased from $4.7 billion to $7.5 billion (U.S.) between 1954 and 1961. Yet French agriculture is probably still far from an optimum production level, in an economic context. In 1955 France's gross agricultural product per capita was half that of the Benelux countries and one-third that of the United States, and the value of gross agricultural output per acre of land was lower than the average for the EEC. Over 75 percent of the farms enumerated in the 1955 census were less than twenty acres in size. Thus large increases in output are possible through the difficult processes of rationalization and consolidation of holdings. They will also come about through the use of more purchased inputs and improvement in the quality of inputs. By 1963–64 France had achieved 110 percent of self-sufficiency in grains, 100 percent in meats, and produced small surpluses of dairy products.

Inquiry into the farm policies of Benelux, West Germany, and Italy is limited largely to their relevance to Canada's trade position. Netherlands agriculture shows the highest productivity rates, as well as the relatively highest per capita income of the rural population, among the EEC members. Her gross agricultural product increased between 1949 and 1961 by 60 percent. Input of farm labour decreased by 20 percent, whereas purchased inputs, including imported feed, increased by 110 percent during the same period.

Analyzing the Dutch economy, Mr. H. Saudie concludes that "agricultural practices in the Netherlands are already so near to the technological optimum that little can be expected from further reduction of that distance to that optimum. . . . As inputs rise faster than outputs, value added will tend to grow very slowly indeed."[3] The Netherlands is the only country where fertilizer input has not increased in recent years. Total funds allocated for agriculture in 1965 were $203 million (U.S.), whereas $217 million was budgeted for 1964. This decline is largely due to reductions in direct subsidies to farmers. All other items of the agricultural budget have been raised, with land development getting the largest increase.

In Belgium the predominance of fragmented farm units characterizes agriculture. The creation of the EEC has encouraged industrial expansion; hence, labour has transferred from agriculture to other sectors of the economy. The number of tractors increased from 12,000 to 60,000 from 1950 to 1963. Nitrogenous fertilizer use increased from 77,000 to 151,000 metric tons. Concurrently, yields of wheat and barley increased from 3,200 to 3,770 kilograms per hectare and from 3,000 to 3,600 kilograms, respectively. Comparable aggregate figures for meat production are 124,000 to 274,000 metric tons.

The Federal Republic of Germany is Canada's most important customer among the Common Market countries. Improved management and a great expansion in the application of purchased inputs have resulted in substantial productivity increase in agriculture (see Table IV). Monthly farm

[3]"Possible Economic Growth in the Netherlands," *Europe's Future in Figures*, Amsterdam, North Holland Publishing Co., 1962, p. 169.

TABLE IV

WEST GERMANY, SELECTED INPUT AND PRODUCTION DATA

Item	1948–52	1965
Number of tractors ('000)	164.1	1,053.2
Fertilizers used ('000 metric tons):		
Nitrogenous	365.0	746.4
Phosphate	405.5	755.7
Potash	660.3	1,125.4
Yield per hectare ('00 kilos):		
Wheat	26.2	35.1
Barley	23.9	31.1
Maize	22.4	36.4
Production ('000 metric tons):		
Meat (except poultry)	1,407	2,964
Poultry meat	42	121

Source: FAO, *Production Yearbook*, no. 18.

wages rose from the equivalent of $16.70 (U.S.) in 1950 to $71.20 in 1963, an increase of 326 percent. The number of paid farm workers was reduced from 885,000 in 1951 to 299,000 in 1963–64, as a result of migration from farms. Non-wage inputs measured in current values almost trebled over the same period.

In Italy, farming was characterized by low outputs and generally by an insufficient use of resources other than labour prior to the land reforms initiated in 1950. The major objective of these reforms was to increase productivity and adjust production patterns to market requirements. EEC policy created comparative advantages for the production of maize, fruits, and vegetables. The government "green plans" also encourage the restriction of wheat production. Generally, the plans have contributed large support for improvement measures, but the amount of these funds has not been published.

The target presented in the Saraceno report is to "create the necessary conditions in agriculture to enable agricultural productivity to match non-agriculture productivity."[4] The report estimates that 150,000 people a year are leaving farms. The number of tractors increased by 431 percent and the use of nitrogenous fertilizers by 158 percent during a recent fifteen-year period. These are modest increases. Taking the average of 1948–53 as a basis of comparison, wheat acreage has declined by about 8 percent, while total output has been practically unchanged. On the other hand, maize yields and total output have increased by 79 and 60 percent, respectively.

[4]Report to Italian Parliament on Italy's Economic Situation, 1963.

This, along with feed grain imports, has provided the basis for doubling meat production.

Community production of meats has not kept up with demand. Self-sufficiency in these products is less today than ten to fifteen years ago. The gap between supply of, and demand for, meat, hard wheat, and fruit has increased sharply. On the other hand, both expansion of quantity and improvement of quality of fruits in Italy and some regions of France have occurred. The expansion of feed grain production and the use of purchased inputs have made possible a rapid increase of livestock production with improvement in quality. But all students of EEC agriculture hold the view that feed grain requirements cannot be met by production within the Community.

Since July 1, 1967, there has been a common market for grain, having all the characteristics of a domestic market. A single levy is imposed on imports of the various cereals from third countries, while intra-Community trade in cereals is free from levies. Refunds or subsidies on intra-Community export trade have been eliminated; for exports, the amount of the subsidy has been unified.

The application of the full levies based on the level of agreed-upon common prices for barley and corn has increased the cost of imports of these grains appreciably. Taking this into account, the Ministers agreed to make an exception for Italy. The levy on barley and corn imported by sea into Italy from third countries has been reduced by $7.50 per metric ton until the end of the 1971–72 marketing year. A special provision has also been made for Durum wheat. This assures producers a price higher than would be obtained on the basis of the agreed target price of $125 per ton.

The results of the foregoing and earlier policies, expressed in terms of output per capita, are presented in Table V. Apart from the Netherlands, the output per capita increased moderately over the seven years

TABLE V

EEC COUNTRIES, INDEX NUMBERS OF TOTAL AGRICULTURAL PRODUCTION PER CAPITA
1956–57 TO 1963–64
(1952–53 to 1956–57 = 100)

Country	1956–57	1957–58	1958–59	1959–60	1960–61	1961–62	1962–63	1963–64
Belgium-Luxembourg	99	105	108	100	109	107	116	116
France	100	99	100	106	116	108	117	113
West Germany	100	101	105	101	113	100	111	114
Italy	102	99	114	112	104	112	110	112
Netherlands	95	101	109	109	109	108	109	105

Source: FAO, *Production Yearbook*, no. 18, p. 34.

from 1956–57 to 1963–64. However, the great bulk of the increase was in livestock and livestock products. Nonetheless, with the rapid increase in demand for these products, the Community was less self-sufficient in 1962–63 than in 1950–53. While incomes have risen sharply in the EEC, they do not seem to have kept pace with family expenditures on food. Thus in West Germany expenditures on food for a typical family of four rose 106 percent from 1950 to 1963, by 25 percent from 1958 to 1963, and by 15 percent from 1960 to 1963.[5] Faced with a comparable situation, France has employed food price controls widely, and they are still in effect. The fact that food accounts for about 35 percent of family living expenditures, compared with 20–23 percent in North America, indicates that western Europe still suffers from high food costs.

The CAP must be regarded as a necessary part of an over-all integration of the six western European economies. The striking industrial achievement of the Community has had an important influence on the agriculture of the area. This is most clearly shown in the change in the composition of diets as a result of higher real incomes. Higher real incomes, the increased cost of marketing services, and increased farm prices have each contributed to the increased retail cost of food. Farm prices have generally risen less than either retail food prices or the cost of living, as indicated in Table VI. To some extent this has been due to the use of a "guided" food and agricultural pricing policy, including the use of consumer subsidies, in all member countries.

TABLE VI

SELECTED COUNTRIES, PERCENTAGE INCREASES IN
SELECTED INDEXES, 1958–64

Country	Farm prices	Retail food prices	Cost of living
France	18	9	8
Germany	11	14	14
Italy	11	17	24
Netherlands	13	22	19
Belgium	14	11	11
Canada	2	8	8
United States	−9	4	7

Source: FAO, *Production Yearbook*, 1965, pp. 432–6.

The widespread use of imported labour in the EEC is well known. This has had an unfavourable influence on the rationalization of agriculture.

[5]H. Hix, "Die Entwicklung der Nahrungsausgaben nach Verbrauchergruppen," *Agrarwirtschaft*, Heft 4, 1965, p. 202.

Were it not for this policy, the increased labour requirements for non-farm industries would have been drawn from the agricultural sector—a type of shift which has been perhaps the most important factor in speeding the rationalization of Canadian agriculture.

The following quotation from Professor John O. Coppock[6] stresses the difficulties of developing a common policy for an industry beset with countless protective devices:

. . . governments have put their national difficulties onto the international bargaining table without showing perceptible interest in "reform" of policies at home. Lacking this interest in taking national action to correct at least part of the international disarray, the discussions within an international framework have no prospect of important success. In this rather futile battle the main importing countries have the best of things. Their domestic agricultural policies may be, and normally are, as economically absurd as those of the exporting countries. . . . By using this (import) control, in conjunction with any of various techniques to tax imports, the net importing countries can sustain their structure of high farm prices internally with little difficulty, if they choose to do so—and most of them have so chosen.

The Common Market has settled most of its internal differences . . . that settlement, however, was wedded to a common policy clearly aimed at greater self-sufficiency with little regard for comparative costs.

Confronted with such an obviously difficult situation for Canadian agriculture, there are, nevertheless, reasons for a restrained optimism. First, continued rapid economic growth in the EEC will lead to a moderate growth in the demand for food through income effects alone. To this must be added population growth. Professor Sol Sinclair states that ". . . the growth of the economy of the EEC, both before and after the CAP, provides an opportunity to increased trade with non-member countries if the latter are willing to make some adjustment."[7] Second, there are already rumblings of discontent about the cost of supporting the farm industry of the EEC. These may increase, particularly if the Community were to suffer a recession of any seriousness, and might result in governmental measures to reduce these costs. In West Germany, France, and Benelux, there is discontent which blames the CAP for high food prices and threatened inflation. Third, to the extent that rationalization measures succeed, the agriculture of the EEC should become more competitive in an international context and thus require less in the way of subsidies. Finally, while the EEC may become a net exporter of wheat, all such exports will be of soft

---

[6]*Atlantic Agricultural Unity: Is It Possible?*, New York, McGraw-Hill, 1966, pp. 17 and 57.
[7]"EEC's Trade in Agricultural Products with Non-member Countries," in *International Journal of Agrarian Affairs*, IV, 5 (1965), p. 287.

wheat. Continued demand for Canadian (and other) hard wheats by the Community is expected, but probably in a declining trend.

Under section 110 of the Treaty of Rome, the EEC is committed to maintaining and expanding international trade. A more positive stricture is included in the provisions of GATT. As contracting parties to GATT, the Six, in forming a customs union, must adopt schedules of duties and other regulations of commerce which "shall not on the whole be higher or more restrictive than the general level of duties and regulations of the commerce" applicable before the customs union was established.[8]

Our final summary statement on the CAP is to emphasize its real costs expressed in a misallocation of resources and of higher food costs. An important aspect of the former is that, with a more liberal trade policy and larger food imports, much of the large investments made in agriculture, as well as a substantial part of current operating expenses, would be available for investment in more productive enterprises. This could clearly affect the capacity of the EEC countries to be competitive in international markets for industrial products.

*Policies of Britain and other European Free Trade
Association (EFTA) countries*

Agriculture is exempted from the EFTA arrangements. Since Britain purchases more than 90 percent of Canada's exports to the Association countries, it is particularly important to consider the farm policies of that country. In 1965 total exports to EFTA countries were $359 million, of which $323 million went to Britain.

Generally the EFTA area developed out of fear among some of the outer seven countries that they would not be able to participate, even economically, in the EEC, but more particularly from a resistance to the original political implications of joining the Community.

The EFTA countries have a total population of 97 million and account for about 10 percent of world income. The countries are highly dependent on international trade, with exports accounting for 23 percent of gross national product. These countries have had a long history of close economic relationship. While the Stockholm Convention excludes farm products from its provisions for tariff reductions, it provides for increasing agricultural trade through bilateral arrangements. This has been of considerable advantage to Denmark and Portugal. Thus, in the early years of the Convention, agricultural products accounted for some 10 percent of total trade within the area. This figure has risen more than one-third—paralleling gains in non-agricultural trade.

[8]GATT, *Basic Instruments and Selected Documents*, III, Geneva, 1958, p. 48.

In postwar Britain the position of agriculture has been guaranteed by the Agricultural Act of 1947. Its basic purpose was to increase the level of self-sufficiency in food from one-third to more than one-half. Warrant for this has been in an appeal to defence policy, general social policy, and to an effort to conserve foreign exchange. The program mechanism has been very largely through deficiency payments. These in recent years have absorbed more than 60 percent of government expenditures on agriculture, which have recently run at $700–$1,000 million per year.

This system does not apply to horticultural crops, which are supported by seasonally variable levies, nor to eggs and milk, for which domestic prices are fixed and the consumer subsidizes the farmer directly. Payments to farmers to assist in making structural improvements (drainage, irrigation, etc.) have taken another 20 percent of total expenditures on agriculture by government, while direct aids, such as fertilizer subsidies, have accounted for some 15 percent. Cost to the government is equivalent to 70 to 80 percent of the net output of the industry. This fact of high support for an inefficient industry, plus the heavy drain on the treasury, has led to misgivings about the policy; over the past several years there has been a determined effort to hold the budgetary line and even to effect cutbacks. Some guaranteed prices have been reduced, and the "standard quantities" to which they apply have been limited. But on the latter it has been difficult to hold the line. However, the cost to the Treasury in 1965 and 1966 was about $700 million, and it was expected to rise to about $780 million in 1967.

Cereals policy is of great importance to Canada. Under a 1960 agreement, minimum import prices have been agreed upon between major export countries. The internal price was $2.04 (Can.) in 1965–66 on domestically produced wheat. Support at the full level of domestic wheat is presently limited to 127 million bushels per year, the standard quantity in the program. Exporting countries compete to fill the annual import quota. Levies are applied to imports other than those from Agreement countries— the levy serves to bring the landed price of imports up to the internal level. Canada is in an advantageous position because of the demand for high-protein wheat. The policy seeks to ensure the import position of traditional foreign suppliers, but in recent years the standard quantities (on which domestic subsidies apply) have been increased to cover increases in domestic requirements.

There has been a steady increase in acreage over the past five years— the 1965 figure exceeded nine million acres. Only if imports threaten to fall significantly below the nine million tons per year imported in the three years before June, 1964, does the government assure remedial action. At the present time the only hopeful notes for Canada's wheat exports to Britain are (1) an ability to bid for a larger share of the rather rigidly limited, and probably declining, total import quota, and (2) the less encouraging prospect for freer trade in the farm products that Britain and Europe import. Canadian wheat exports to Britain have already been declining, and it is not unlikely that Britain will within a year or two request a reduction in the nine-million-ton over-all import quota. Changing technology in the baking industry detracts from the advantage held by Canadian hard red wheats—and this could become a serious problem for Canada, not only in the British market, but in all her export markets. The implications of Britain's possible entry into the EEC will be considered later.

Canadian cheddar cheese, once a major Canadian export to Britain, is now exported in modest quantities, 20 to 30 million pounds a year, but under an export subsidy. It commands a 10 to 12 percent premium over pasteurized cheddars produced in New Zealand and England. Its position in the British market will become increasingly secure as British incomes rise. Apple exports from Canada to Britain, very important in the pre-1939 period, are now faced with an eighty-thousand-ton import quota from all dollar countries. Canada has been filling an increasing proportion of the quota. If Britain should overcome her balance of payments difficulties, the prospect for apple exports would be good.

As noted earlier, Britain is making a determined effort to rationalize her agriculture. This is regarded as a necessary aspect of her traditional cheap (at retail levels) food policy. Without substantial improvement in productivity, costs to the government could mount to clearly unacceptable levels. While output per worker increased by 6 percent per year (1960–64), this was achieved by means of heavy new investments—thus injuring in some measure other industries requiring capital. Even in the face of this encouraging improvement in labour productivity, when considered against the postwar experience of major agricultural exporters, it appears that Britain has lost ground relatively over the entire postwar period.

In the other EFTA countries—in fact, for the whole area—it is clear that over-all gains could be secured from freer trade in farm products. All employ tariffs and/or quantitative restraints, though these are practically non-existent in Denmark. Efforts to support farm incomes in that country have been pursued increasingly, though not by import restraints. In the Scandinavian countries, the emphasis of farm policy is on aiding families on small farms—and is thus just as much or more a matter of social as of agricultural policy. On the whole, Sweden, Switzerland, and Denmark have followed relatively liberal policies vis-à-vis their EFTA partners on agricultural products. Austria, Norway, and Finland have tended to be more protectionist, and their imports of farm products have increased little over the years this economic area has been in existence.

Denmark and Austria have been anxious to join the EEC if the terms were right; and, in fact, Austria has begun negotiations. Norway has also made overtures in that direction. Switzerland shows no enthusiasm for joining, while the position of Finland, because of her special relationship to Russia, is most uncertain.[9] But if Britain or Britain, Austria, and Denmark should join the EEC, EFTA would cease to have much economic meaning, and the other countries might be forced into some kind of associate membership.

Policies of the United States

While barriers to international trade in agricultural products were implicitly a part of the American agricultural adjustment legislation of the early 1930s, they did not become really serious until after the Second World War. Then the Havana Charter, which became the basis for GATT, clearly established exceptional treatment for agricultural products. This document, drafted in Washington, justified the use of export subsidies and import restrictions on farm products. Thus, more than any country up to that time, the United States placed agricultural products outside the scope of GATT negotiations. The "necessity" for such interventions arose from the United States' choosing (as the EEC has done in recent years) to protect farm incomes through supporting farm prices.

In briefest terms, for more than thirty years the United States has attempted to secure the income gains which would come from restriction of output of products whose demand is inelastic. And during the whole period the success of these measures has been frustrated by the slow growth of demand, by the advance of technology, and by structural changes in the industry. Even with vigorous efforts to restrain production, it has increased year by year, while farm prices in 1964 were below 1957–59 levels. But as noted elsewhere, 1965 and 1966 have seen significant increases in farm prices—and these may be sustained or even further increased. However, recent gains are due more to American economic development and to events abroad than to the farm policies of the United States.

The current programs in the United States had their origin in the Agricultural Act of 1933, which provided acreage allotments and price supports for "basic" farm products: wheat, corn, cotton, rice, tobacco, and peanuts. This was, and is, known as the "parity" program, since its

[9]See S. J. Wells, "EFTA—The End of the Transition," *Lloyds Bank Review,* no. 82, Oct. 1966, pp. 18–33.

objective was to bring the prices of these products into a farm-purchasing-power-parity relationship with the period 1910–14. Special land-use and rural-welfare programs were begun soon after 1933. Surpluses continued in the 1930s, but these became a national blessing during the Second World War. They appeared again in the late 1940s, and while some disappeared in the Korean War period, they became serious by 1954. In that year the surplus disposal law (the Agricultural Trade Development and Assistance Act, PL480), was passed, and within two years 40 percent of U.S. farm exports were moving under that program.[10] Continued difficulties from surpluses and low prices led to the Soil Bank program, begun in 1956. This provided for payments equivalent to rent for fifty to sixty million acres put in a conservation reserve and not cropped. During the later Eisenhower years, reduction in price supports on wheat and feed grains was accompanied by some general relaxation of production controls, and surpluses again became a serious problem, despite sales under PL480.

The policy developments which had been under way gradually for nearly a decade were formalized and extended in the Food and Agriculture Act of 1965. The emphasis in this legislation is on extending a two-price system, with high price supports limited to that part of production required for domestic consumption. For instance, the basic loan or support level in the case of wheat is $1.25 per bushel, which makes American wheat fully competitive in world markets. Domestic consumption of wheat is subsidized to the extent of $1.32 per bushel. Thus, in reality, a large export subsidy continues under the new program. The essence of the new arrangement is to substitute aggressive American competition in foreign markets for a policy of holding large commodity stocks in the hands of the government.

Accompanying these changes in domestic agricultural programs, the Food for Freedom Act of 1966 made generally consistent changes in the American food-aid and surplus-disposal operations. Emphasis was placed on expanding international trade in farm products, implicitly on a commercial basis. Local currency sales, which over the past ten years have accounted for almost two-thirds of all PL480 exports, are to be very largely phased out by 1971, by which time almost all concessional sales will be on the basis of long-term loans.

So much for a general overview intended to present the broadest outline of the American problem and policies over the years since 1945. The background of the problem rests not only in the cruelly distressing farm situation of the depression of the 1930s, but more deeply in history, and

[10]The Act provides for four types of programs. Title I covers sales for foreign currencies; Title II covers famine and relief; Title III includes domestic donations; and Title IV, long-term credit sales.

in the nature of agricultural development reflecting the particular resource and market problems of the American farmer. There was rural poverty in wide areas, the fluctuations of farm prices and incomes were erratic, and the gap in the living standards between the rural and the urban populations was extreme.

The United States is the world's largest exporter of agricultural commodities. Agricultural products account for about one-quarter of total U.S. exports. Several of its crops depend heavily on the export market. However, in general, the importance of farm exports and the range of commodities involved reflect much more the failure of crop-restriction programs than the comparative advantages of the various sectors of the industry.

The major crop exports and the percentage of total production of each important export in the 1965/66 fiscal year are presented in Table VII. The United States also had substantial exports of fruits and fruit preparations ($327 million), dairy products ($174 million), oilcake and meal ($216 million), tallow ($159 million), vegetables and preparations ($170 million), hides and skins ($139 million), poultry products ($72 million), variety meats ($56 million), and lard ($23 million). Total agricultural exports of the United States in the fiscal year 1965/66 were $6,681 million. This is the highest figure on record. Over the earlier years of the decade, agricultural exports varied from $4,517 million to $6,096 million.

While the U.S. government describes exports other than those under PL480 as commercial, moderate to large-scale subsidies have continued to

TABLE VII

UNITED STATES, AGRICULTURAL EXPORTS, 1965/66 FISCAL YEAR

	Exports			Percentage of crop exported under PL480 and AID*
Crop	Quantity (millions)	Value (mil. $)	Percentage of crop exported	
Wheat and wheat flour	859 bus.	1,403	67	67
Feed grains	25.9 met. tons	1,383	47	9
Soybeans	257 bus.	734	30	1
Cotton	3.1 bales	386	20	26
Tobacco	472 lb.	395		27
Soybean and cottonseed oil	1,390 lb.	189	18	68
Rice	30.4 bags	222	48	32

Source: United States, Department of Agriculture, *Export Fact Sheet* and *Import Fact Sheet*, 1966.

*Agency for International Development.

apply to most of the price-supported products moving into competitive world markets.[11] Table VIII shows the unit and total subsidies required to move a selected group of commodities into commercial export markets in the fiscal year 1963/64. These, of course, are over and above PL480 subsidies. It will be noted that meats and livestock products (except dairy products) and fruits and vegetables are not included in Table VIII. Thus exports of these products are truly commercial.

TABLE VIII

UNITED STATES, EXPORT SUBSIDIES, 1963/64 FISCAL YEAR

Commodity	Unit	Payment per unit ($)	Payment total (mil. $)
Wheat and flour	bushel	.56	427
Cotton	bale	42.50	219
Rice	cwt.	2.28	71
Milk, non-fat, dry	pound	.082	55
Butter	pound	.34	35
Milkfat	pound	.42	5
Cheese	pound	.16	
Tobacco	pound	.193	3
Flaxseed	pound	.06	*
Peanuts	pound	.07	4
Total			820

Source: *International Federation of Agricultural Producers News,*
July 1965, p. 3.
*Less than 0.5.

American farm exports do not clearly reflect the comparative-advantage position of the industry. Nor do production trends reflect domestic needs. Crop output in the United States has been increasing, in recent years, twice as rapidly as consumption of farm products. Although the prospect of overproduction has been moderated by phenomenal export demands (largely food for the developing countries), it will probably continue to be a problem. In addition to this, the oversupply of farmers and the trend to increased productivity in U.S. agriculture will aggravate the situation.

An examination of productivity trends in American agriculture indicates

[11]U.S. government publications euphemistically describe "commercial sales" as including "in addition to unassisted commercial transactions, shipments of some commodities with governmental assistance in the form of (1) credits for relatively short periods; (2) sales of government-owned commodities at less than domestic market prices; and (3) export payments in cash and kind." United States, Department of Agriculture, *Export Fact Sheet* and *Import Fact Sheet*, 1966. These subsidies have been employed on a very large scale over the past fifteen years.

tremendous advances over the past twenty years. Total production increased from an index value of 87 in 1949 to 115 in 1965 (1957–59 = 100), while total inputs showed almost no change. The composition and the quality of inputs, however, have been changing rapidly. This reflects the relative decline in the costs of farm inputs derived from the non-farm industrial sector, as compared with the wages of labour. Over the past fifteen years, relative to the cost of farm labour, the cost of fertilizer has dropped by 70 percent, that of farm machinery by 50 percent, and that of all capital inputs by 59 percent.[12]

TABLE IX

UNITED STATES, INDEX NUMBERS OF MAJOR INPUTS, 1949–64
(1957–59 = 100)

Year	Total input	Farm labour	Farm real estate	Mechanical power and machinery	Fertilizer and lime	Feed, seed, and livestock purchases*	Miscel- laneous
1949	101	152	95	80	61	69	82
1950	101	142	97	86	68	72	85
1951	104	143	98	92	73	80	88
1952	103	136	99	96	80	81	88
1953	103	131	99	97	83	80	91
1954	102	125	100	98	88	82	91
1955	102	120	100	99	90	86	94
1956	101	113	99	99	91	91	98
1957	99	104	100	100	94	93	95
1958	99	99	100	99	97	101	100
1959	102	97	100	101	109	106	105
1960	101	92	100	100	110	109	106
1961	101	89	100	99	114	123	109
1962	101	85	100	96	124	121	113
1963	102	83	101	99	132	124	115
1964	103	81	102	101	137	123	120

Source: *Economic Report of the President*, Washington, D.C., U.S. Government Printing Office, 1965, p. 279.
*Non-farm portion of feed, seed, and livestock purchases.

Thus the total labour input in American agriculture declined by 47 percent from 1949 to 1964; power and machinery inputs increased by 26 percent; fertilizer and lime, by 125 percent; purchased feed, seed, and livestock inputs, by 78 percent; and miscellaneous inputs, by 46 percent. These data are presented in Table IX. Accompanying these changes, the

[12]*U.S. Agriculture in 1980*, Ames, Iowa State University, 1966, p. 6.

number of farms declined by an estimated 40 percent, while the size of farms roughly doubled.

The consequences of the developments described may be summarized in terms of changes in productivity. The appropriate data are presented in Table X.

TABLE X

UNITED STATES, FARM OUTPUT PER
UNIT OF INPUT, 1949–65
(1957–59 = 100)

Year	Productivity index
1949–52	86
1953–56	93
1957–60	101
1961	106
1962	107
1963	110
1964	109
1965	112

Source: U.S., Department of Agriculture, *Agricultural Statistics*, 1965, p. 458, and earlier issues of the same annual.

While the productivity gains are modest—less than 2 percent per year—they are not unimpressive, considering that farm prices were depressed under the pressure of large surpluses during most of the period. (These productivity measures are all in deflated value terms.) However, when considered on the basis of labour productivity, the gains are much more striking. Over the period from 1949 to 1965, farm output per man-hour increased by 168 percent. This large increase of labour productivity indicates unmistakably the revolutionary changes occurring in the agricultural industries.

The changes which have occurred in American agriculture must be regarded as one of the most important economic phenomena of the postwar years. This statement is made in the context that even without export subsidies the vast surplus-producing agricultural industry of the United States will press its output on every world market and will probably increasingly expose the high economic and social costs involved in agricultural protectionism in Britain, western Europe, and other countries—including Canada.

There is little doubt that the pace of economic change which has transformed American agriculture in the postwar years will not only continue but will accelerate. Education, communication, and mobility among the regional and economic sectors are becoming more effective. Agriculture, once intractable, has become knowledgeable about, and acclimated to, the process of economic growth. And competition within the industry is gathering momentum as resources move into the hands of stronger managers.[13] Capital now represents 75 percent of all inputs, and it is projected that this figure will rise to 90 percent in twenty years or less. The Iowa study projects a decline of more than 50 percent in numbers of farmers and about 40 percent in the farm labour force by 1980. It also projects that the agriculture of 1980 could still produce large surpluses over domestic requirements.

The important implications that past and projected changes in the structure of American agriculture hold for prospects in agricultural trade are considered in a later chapter.

Canadian agricultural development and policies

Reference has been made to the extent and importance of agricultural exports in the Canadian economy and also to the relatively strong comparative advantage of Canadian agriculture in several important commodities. We turn now to an examination of the structure of the industry and of how structural changes may strengthen the position of agriculture in a world trade context.

In the period 1951–61, the amount of improved acreage in farmland increased by 7 percent, from 96.9 million acres to 103.4 million. This was mainly the result of an 11 percent expansion in the Prairie provinces. During the same period there was a decrease in the Maritimes, Quebec, and Ontario of 22, 11, and 5 percent, respectively. British Columbia increased improved acreage by 14 percent. With a large decline in the numbers of farms over the decade,[14] the average size of farms, as indicated in Table XI, increased very substantially—more than one-third for Canada as a whole. This by itself would obviously greatly strengthen the position of the farm industry, beset as it has historically been by problems of small scale and inadequate capitalization.

In a broad sense the relative strength of the agriculture of the various regions of Canada is revealed by measures showing the proportion of farm units which are too small or inadequately capitalized to allow efficient production. By an arbitrary definition it may be assumed that an adequately

[13]See *ibid.*
[14]Fourteen percent for Canada, based on the 1951 definition of a farm; 25 percent for the Atlantic provinces, 19 percent for Quebec, 20 percent for Ontario, 16 percent in the Prairie provinces, and 9 percent in British Columbia.

TABLE XI

CANADA AND REGIONS, AVERAGE SIZE OF FARMS
(acres)

Region	Total land			Improved land		
	1951	1961	Percentage change 1951–61	1951	1961	Percentage change 1951–61
Atlantic	123	132	7	37	55	49
Quebec	125	140	12	66	82	24
Ontario	139	149	7	85	99	14
Prairies	498	609	22	288	384	33
British Columbia	178	194	9	44	65	48
Canada	279	336	20	156	215	38

Source: *U.S. Census of Agriculture* and S. H. Lane, "Recent and Comparative Changes in Canadian Agriculture," Canadian Agricultural Economics Society, *Workshop Report*, 1963, p. 11.

TABLE XII

CANADA AND REGIONS, PERCENTAGE OF FARMS WITH ANNUAL SALES OF
$10,000 OR MORE, AND PERCENTAGE OF AGRICULTURAL OUTPUT
FROM SUCH FARMS, 1958

Region	Percentage of farms with annual sales of $10,000 or more	Sales by these farms as percentage of sales by all farms
Maritimes	3	20
Quebec	5	22
Ontario	14	45
Prairies	9	32
British Columbia	9	48
Canada	9	34

Source: J. M. Fitzpatrick and C. V. Parker, "Distribution of Income in Canadian Agriculture," p. 5 (mimeo).

capitalized farm might have annual sales of $10,000 or more. The proportion of census farms and the percentage of total farm sales in this category in 1958 are shown in Table XII. Thus only a small proportion of Canadian farms (from 3 to 14 percent, depending on the region) are adequately capitalized by this definition, and from 20 to 48 percent of agricultural output comes from such farms. The data reveal an important feature of the Canadian farm industry—the comparatively large output produced by the largest 9 percent of the farms. With size of farms increasing rapidly since 1958, the 9 percent largest farms at the present time would probably account for well over 40 percent of total sales.

Between 1951 and 1964, the labour force employed in agriculture declined by one-third, from 939,000 to 630,000, and accounted for less than 10 percent of the total labour force in 1964.[15] The downward trend took place in all provinces. The greatest reduction in the farm labour force was in Quebec, where it amounted to some 50 percent. Next was the Maritime provinces, with a 39 percent reduction. In Ontario, the Prairie region, and British Columbia, the labour force was reduced by 33, 23, and 21 percent, respectively.

The rate of decline is highly dependent on the nearby non-agriculture employment opportunities and on the rate at which mechanization of farm production increases. More people have left agriculture in regions where alternative job opportunities were available. According to Professor Lane, "Regionally, we find that Ontario and British Columbia offered the greatest opportunities for new employment during the decade 1951–61. Although there was an absolute growth in employment in the Prairie region during this period, the rate of growth was less than the national average."[16]

Capital inputs in agriculture may be divided into two groups, capital investments and operating expenses (exclusive of labour).

Table XIII shows the changes which took place in machinery and equipment investment between 1951 and 1961. The number of tractors increased by 30 percent in Canada. In general, the increase was greater in eastern Canada than in the West. The number of trucks used for farm purposes rose 54 percent in Canada during the same period. The number of grain combines increased by 72 percent. The increase in the Prairie provinces, although smaller than in the eastern provinces, was still very significant. In Manitoba and Saskatchewan the number of grain combines increased by 55 and 51 percent, respectively, whereas in Alberta the number rose by 85 percent.

In the same period, the number of electric motors increased by 126 percent, the largest increase taking place in the Prairie provinces. In 1961, the number of electrified farms in Canada was reported at 409,882. The percentage of farms making use of electric power in 1951 and in 1961 is shown by province in Table XIV.

As in other countries, the increase in purchased inputs is one of the most significant structural changes in agriculture in the postwar period. Purchased inputs are measured for Canada by the cash operating-expense

[15]Dominion Bureau of Statistics, *The Labour Force*, April 1965.
[16]Lane, "Recent and Comparative Changes in Canadian Agriculture," pp. 10, 12.

TABLE XIII

CANADA AND REGIONS, NUMBER OF FARM MACHINES AND EQUIPMENT, 1951 AND 1961

Item	Year	Maritimes	Quebec	Ontario	Prairie provinces	British Columbia	Canada
Automobiles	1951	19,288	41,602	114,870	141,337	12,557	329,667
	1961	18,526	55,385	110,773	158,938	14,322	357,944
Trucks	1951	12,650	19,167	41,486	113,512	9,291	196,122
	1961	14,590	26,597	62,812	185,983	12,004	302,012
Tractors	1951	12,430	31,971	105,204	236,930	13,148	399,683
	1961	4,351	70,697	150,046	290,700	16,974	549,789
Combines	1951	245	420	10,031	79,117	687	90,500
	1961	1,570	3,046	22,387	127,276	1,331	155,611
Balers	1951	—	—	—	—	—	—
	1961	4,081	13,212	28,061	41,488	2,679	89,522
Forage harvesters	1951	—	—	—	—	—	—
	1961	396	1,551	8,945	4,663	1,208	16,764
Milking machines	1951	4,188	17,632	37,464	8,770	3,129	70,883
	1961	6,553	34,724	44,284	17,191	3,365	106,119

Source: DBS, *Census of Agriculture*, 1951 and 1961.

TABLE XIV

CANADA AND REGIONS, PERCENTAGE OF FARMS
USING ELECTRIC POWER, 1951 AND 1961

Area	1951	1961
Newfoundland	38	66
Nova Scotia	71	91
Prince Edward Island	22	78
New Brunswick	60	96
Quebec	67	97
Ontario	74	95
Manitoba	48	90
Saskatchewan	16	66
Alberta	25	72
British Columbia	59	87
Canada	51	85

Source: Calculated from DBS, *Census of Agriculture*, 1951 and 1961.

item in DBS farm net income statistics. They increased by 63 percent from 1951 to 1964, while cash income from farming operations increased by only 22 percent. In fact, cash operating expenses now take up 85 and 83 percent of cash farm income in Nova Scotia and New Brunswick (Table XV). This leaves only 15 and 17 percent of cash income to be set against depreciation charges, interest on owned capital, and labour and management return—obviously entirely inadequate.

TABLE XV

CANADA AND REGIONS, OPERATING COSTS AS PERCENTAGE OF
CASH FARM RECEIPTS, 1951–64

Area	1951–54	1955–58	1959–61	1962–64
Prince Edward Island	55	61	66	72
Nova Scotia	86	76	80	85
New Brunswick	69	69	75	83
Quebec	54	64	71	70
Ontario	48	60	66	66
Manitoba	42	51	50	51
Saskatchewan	39	45	43	42
Alberta	43	46	46	49
British Columbia	71	62	63	59
Canada	47	54	57	57

Source: Compiled from DBS, *Quarterly Bulletin of Agricultural Statistics*, various numbers.

One of the largest inputs included in operating costs is fertilizer. Table XVI shows the fertilizer expenditures in constant dollars (1935–39 = 100) between 1951 and 1964. Total expenditures on fertilizer between the periods 1951–54 and 1962–64 increased by 84 percent; the most significant increases took place in Alberta, Saskatchewan, and British Columbia. In Alberta the fertilizer input in real terms rose by 340 percent; in Saskatchewan, by 146 percent; and in British Columbia, by 105 percent. The lowest increases occurred in the Maritime provinces.

TABLE XVI

CANADA AND REGIONS, FERTILIZER EXPENDITURES, 1951–64

Area	1951–54	1955–58	1959–61	1962–64	Percentage increase 1951–54 to 1962–64
Prince Edward Island	1,390	1,650	1,648	1,686	21
Nova Scotia	1,023	924	967	1,100	8
New Brunswick	2,200	2,085	2,182	2,237	2
Quebec	4,426	5,054	6,872	8,136	84
Ontario	13,600	15,755	18,242	24,099	77
Manitoba	1,597	976	1,506	2,450	43
Saskatchewan	1,839	1,249	2,052	4,518	146
Alberta	1,955	2,051	4,230	8,596	340
British Columbia	1,337	1,577	2,029	2,536	105
Canada	29,075	31,111	38,955	53,544	84

Source: Computed from farm income data in DBS, *Quarterly Bulletin of Agricultural Statistics*, various numbers.

The number of milk cows changed little over the period 1951 to 1964. A slight downward trend is evident in the Maritime provinces, Manitoba, and Saskatchewan, offset by a small upward trend in Quebec and British Columbia. Cattle other than milk cows show a definite increase in Canada. From just over five million head in 1951, the number increased to over nine million head in 1964. The most significant increase took place in the Prairie provinces, where the number has more than doubled since 1951. However, upward trends are also shown in the other provinces. The number of hogs, although fluctuating cyclically, has been fairly constant since 1951. The small number of sheep in Canada has also changed very little since 1951.

In an important work on the changing input structure and productivity of Canadian agriculture,[17] I. F. Furniss provides measures respecting eight

[17]"Productivity Trends in Canadian Agriculture, 1935–64," *Canadian Farm Economics*, vol. I, no. 1 (1966).

TABLE XVII

INDEXES OF INPUTS, BY SELECTED CATEGORIES, 1939-65
(1949 = 100)

			Capital							
Year	Real estate*	Labour†	Machinery and equipment‡	Livestock§	Purchased feed and seed	Fertilizer and limestone	Electric power	Miscellaneous∥	Total capital	Total inputs
1935-39	112	137	52	102	41	34	22	61	53	106
1945	99.4	99.1	77.0	118.4	106.7	75.3	40.6	67.2	87.5	95.5
1946	103.3	110.1	82.4	114.8	125.3	80.5	53.1	87.0	97.5	104.8
1947	102.7	104.2	87.4	110.1	147.7	87.7	63.9	99.2	107.6	105.0
1948	101.3	101.8	93.2	91.4	108.0	89.5	82.3	103.5	98.1	100.5
1949	100.0	100.0	100.0	100.0	100.0	100.0	100.0	100.0	100.0	100.0
1950	98.3	94.5	114.5	101.1	93.5	102.4	128.4	98.7	105.4	98.7
1951	96.9	87.2	110.6	115.5	95.0	106.2	153.0	95.3	105.0	94.8
1952	96.6	82.7	115.0	124.9	93.4	101.4	173.4	91.4	107.0	93.2
1953	102.0	79.7	122.5	114.6	89.8	115.2	199.3	87.9	109.1	93.4
1954	101.9	81.5	123.5	108.3	102.5	110.6	228.2	87.6	112.7	95.4
1955	103.9	76.0	125.0	116.2	100.7	106.0	247.6	94.8	114.2	93.6
1956	104.2	72.1	124.8	112.7	121.1	109.2	274.5	97.5	120.2	93.7
1957	102.7	69.4	124.3	114.3	114.4	111.4	297.6	90.8	117.8	91.3
1958	107.3	66.7	123.1	132.0	139.4	120.6	318.9	89.9	126.1	93.5
1959	109.6	65.0	124.4	140.6	139.2	132.6	342.6	98.2	128.8	94.0
1960	110.8	63.4	126.4	138.4	136.0	134.4	354.4	101.2	129.1	93.5
1961	111.9	63.2	123.1	143.9	131.3	154.5	369.3	108.8	128.3	93.4
1962	114.2	61.3	128.7	139.8	131.5	168.0	403.0	108.8	131.5	93.9
1963	114.4	60.2	133.2	149.7	141.9	188.5	421.8	118.5	139.3	96.0
1964	114.0	58.5	136.9	158.3	150.2	225.4	435.3	123.0	146.2	97.2
1965	115.6	55.2	141.2	142.0	164.7	243.2	458.3	118.9	151.6	97.6

*Includes interest on investment, depreciation and repairs on buildings, and property taxes, all for both owned and rented real estate.

†Total farm labour force (farm operators, unpaid family labour, and hired labour).

‡Includes fuel and other purchased items associated with machinery operation plus interest on investment and depreciation.

§Interest on investment in livestock and purchased livestock.

inputs. His data are presented in Table XVII. They show labour input to have been reduced nearly 50 percent since the first postwar quinquennium. Total capital inputs rose by a similar proportion over the same period. Among the capital inputs, fertilizer increased about 165 percent. This is one of the most significant structural changes in Canadian agriculture. While the percentage increase in the input of electricity is considerably greater, this particular input still accounts for a very small part of total inputs. The study cited shows that labour now accounts for about 30 percent of total inputs, down from 50 percent in the 1945–49 period. On the other hand, total capital inputs now represent about one-half of all inputs, up from 30 percent in 1945–49. This switch in relative importance of these groups of inputs, paralleling that of the United States, measures the modernization of the farm industry. This trend will continue, its rapidity depending on the rate of growth of the non-farm economy. As it proceeds, agriculture will become more commercial in character and less oriented to the labour of the family farm.

The increased importance of capital inputs, especially fertilizer, has resulted in apparent increases in yields per acre. The relevant data are presented in Table XVIII. However, one must take account of the fact

TABLE XVIII

YIELDS PER ACRE, SELECTED CROPS,
ANNUAL AVERAGES, 1926–55 AND 1956–64
(bushels per acre)

Crop	1926–55	1956–64
Wheat	16.6	20.0
Oats	30.6	40.7
Barley	23.8	28.2
Rye	13.2	16.5

Source: DBS, *Handbook of Agricultural Statistics* and *Quarterly Bulletin of Agricultural Statistics*

that weather conditions were more favourable in the latter period. In fact, one is surprised by the relatively smaller yield increases in Canada, compared with those of the United States. This clearly reflects on the relative strength of the agriculture of the two countries and represents a major challenge to Canadian farmers and equally to the scientific programs on which they depend for higher yields.

W. M. Drummond and William MacKenzie[18] found, for the period

[18]*Progress and Prospects for Canadian Agriculture*, Ottawa, Queen's Printer, 1958, p. 84.

1935–39 to 1955, an increase of about 24 percent in output per hog and of about 26 percent for beef. In the present research, it has been impossible to secure fully comparable data. However, preliminary work suggests a continuation of productivity gains, but at a slightly lower rate (see Table XIX).

TABLE XIX

CANADA, PRODUCTIVITY IN
AGRICULTURE, 1953–64
(constant 1949 dollars per man-hour)

Year	Productivity
1953	0.98
1954	0.76
1955	0.99
1960	0.91
1961	0.82
1962	1.13
1963	1.30
1964	1.25

Source: 1953–55 data: Hood and Scott, *Output, Labour and Capital in the Canadian Economy*, p. 399; 1960–64 data: rough extension of Hood and Scott data by authors of present study (see text).

William Hood and Anthony Scott, in their constant-dollar estimates (1949 dollars) of gross domestic product in Canadian agriculture over the period 1926–55, found that productivity measured in constant 1949 dollars per man-hour rose from $0.58 to $0.99 over the years 1946–55.[19] This is a good measure of the results of the sweeping structural changes in Canadian agriculture over these years. We have attempted an extension of this measure, although the result must necessarily be rough, since data on hours of work per week or per man-year are not available. We have arbitrarily estimated that farm labour works fifty-five hours per week, fifty weeks per year. The results are shown in Table XIX.

A generally comparable measure for the United States was presented earlier in this study. It showed a 168 percent increase in product per man-hour from 1949 through 1965. Over those years American agriculture became relatively more capital-intensive. This in part accounts for the

[19]*Output, Labour and Capital in the Canadian Economy*, Royal Commission on Canada's Economic Prospects, Ottawa, 1955, chap. v, Appendix F.

above results. Further, the U.S. industry was only partially exposed to the forces of world competition. In terms of over-all productivity Canadian agriculture shows up very well. Furniss shows that in terms of value output per unit of composite input, Canadian farm productivity increased at a compound rate of more than 2 percent per year over the past fifteen years, while that of the United States increased at a rate of less than 2 percent per year. The low rate of gain reflects more than anything else the fact that farm product prices in both countries were unresponsive to economic development.

In any assessment of Canada's prospective position in international markets, wheat is naturally of major importance. This fact has both favourable and unfavourable features. Each of the last five crops was extremely large and would normally result in marketing difficulties. However, these large crops coincided with the very large-scale entry of the USSR, China, and eastern European countries into the Canadian market. In fact, in Canada's booming export trade in 1964, wheat was our largest export, and most of that went to the areas named above. Thus, year-end carry-over has not developed into a serious problem. It would have been extremely serious were it not for purchases by the Communist countries.

The trend of exports to traditional markets in western Europe and Japan has been slowly declining for the past five years. This is a serious matter, since the prospect is that the decline may continue and even be accelerated by technological developments in milling that apparently will detract from the advantage of Canada's high-protein wheat. In these markets, Canada has been faced with competition of subsidized American wheat, with surpluses of French wheat looking for a home, and with governmental pressures on western European and British millers to use a smaller proportion of Canadian wheat in flour mixes.

In addition, the Communist countries are under tremendous pressure to reach a state of self-sufficiency in food grains, and they clearly have the land resources to realize this. The prospect is that over the next five to ten years most of these countries will reach self-sufficiency, or at least will not provide the very large markets they have in recent years. Thus, over the longer period, Canada may face increasing difficulties in marketing large wheat crops.

Canada's shipments of wheat to the developing countries, both in an external-aid and in a commercial-sales context, have increased sharply. The prospect is that the demand for food grains in both spheres will increase rapidly. On the one hand, nothing could stimulate commercial wheat exports more rapidly than well-based economic development. On the other, if these countries fail to secure economic development and at the same time experience rapid population growth, the need for foreign aid will increasingly take the form of food-grain shipments. Both will assuredly be of great importance over the next decade or two. Further, oilseed crops are coming to occupy an increasingly important role in Canadian agriculture. The 1966 acreage of 3.7 million was the highest on record, and there is evidence that the improvement in production technology in Canada will make these crops increasingly competitive in international trade. With a moderate expansion of the demand for livestock products on this continent, it is our judgment that the wheat area of Canadian agriculture can make the prospective adjustments (favourable or unfavourable) which may face this sector of agriculture.

The only other important sector of Canadian agriculture which faces possible significant adjustment in the light of international trade considerations is the dairy industry. Of course, the fluid sector of the industry, which uses nearly 40 percent of the milk leaving farms, is protected by a tangle of provincial and municipal restraints. Butter production, which takes up more than 30 percent of total milk production, is exceedingly inefficient, and returns to labour and capital are generally very low despite a butter price roughly twice that in competitive world markets. In cheddar cheese, on the other hand, Canada has a clear and large comparative advantage but is restrained by the virtual prohibition on exports to the United States and by restraints imposed by other countries. However, with some relaxation of trade barriers and the resultant diversion of manufacturing milk from butter to cheese, most of the difficulties would disappear. Judging by the cost of present producer and consumer subsidies to manufacturing milk, Canada could afford to make substantial concessions to secure wider markets for cheddar cheese.

Certainly the present maze of municipal, provincial, and federal restraints and subsidies, whose incidence can be seen only dimly, is neither conveying adequate returns to farmers nor assisting in the needed adjustments of the industry. It is significant that the United States, faced with a similar market situation and an equally inelastic supply, has increasingly (and with success) turned these problems over to the market.

The development of Canadian agriculture reflects in no small degree the types of farm policy which have been embraced by the country. In its historical context, policy was largely concerned with the conquest and settlement of the Prairie frontier area, with the provision of rail transport services involving special tariffs for export grains, and with the restricting influences on agricultural development of the national (tariff) policy beginning in 1879.

In the first four decades of the present century—until the Second World War—emphasis in farm policy was on (1) maintaining a market economy in the agricultural sector, (2) education, extension, and research—all in the public sector, (3) public provision of farm credit, with the purpose of strengthening the family farm, (4) grading and inspection services and public assistance in the provision of warehousing and processing facilities, and (5) aids to the cooperative movement and authorization of the creation of provincially oriented marketing boards.

Such policies made only limited contributions to raising or stabilizing farm incomes. Thus, policies of the 1930s and the post-1939 period put emphasis on these areas. In 1935 the monopoly Canadian Wheat Board was created, a modest crop-insurance scheme for Prairie farmers was inaugurated, and, after the war, price supports on an increasing range of products were introduced. To these measures has been added the Agricultural Rehabilitation and Development program (ARDA), the purpose of which is to lead the way in land and human-resource adjustment in the chronically low-income areas of Canadian agriculture.

As in the United States, farm income has not responded to the fairly rigorous policies employed. In fact, the real income of the industry fell substantially throughout more than a decade of the 1950s and into the 1960s. The consequences were moderated when viewed on the basis of the farm family and entirely overcome when considered on a per worker basis. But at the same time real incomes of non-farm workers were rising substantially. However, as noted earlier, when incomes of farm people from non-farm sources are included, the situation of farm families is shown to be significantly improved.

Canadian agriculture has clearly suffered from the restrictive Canadian trade policies and those of actual and potential importers. Even the most protected sector, the dairy industry, produces very low incomes per worker. And typically incomes have been highest in the export sectors of the Canadian farm industry. On the cost side, the industry's comparative-advantage position is worsened by the tariff on some types of agricultural equipment, on corn, and on other feeds. This suggests that revision of tariff policy would be to the advantage of Canadian agriculture—even if the adjustments were made on a unilateral basis.

We must accept the judgment of Dr. John A. Dawson[20] that, compared to other major agricultural countries, the performance of Canadian agriculture has been very satisfactory. Dawson's main point is that Canadian policy, with relatively minor supports for farm prices and income, has permitted rapid structural adjustments, essentially in a market context. At the same time he is aware that the low incomes in large sectors of Canadian agriculture represent an important policy problem.

[20]"The Performance of Canadian Agriculture," *Agricultural Institute Reviewer*, XXI, May–June 1966, p. 18.

IV. Possibilities and Strategy for Freer Trade

In this exceedingly difficult area, consideration must be given to the prospects for achieving freer trade in farm products by any of the following means, or by combinations of means: (1) multilateral GATT negotiations; (2) the development of additional blocs, or groups such as the EEC, EFTA, Comecon, or the Latin American Free Trade Area; (3) the prospect that the continuing improvement in cost-price relationships, especially in North American agriculture, will make possible, or even require, relaxation of quantitative import controls and make domestic farm aid programs less needed and less costly; (4) further erosion of British preferences; (5) unilateral tariff reduction by individual countries; (6) reductions in barriers of a non-tariff, non-quota character; (7) the development of a commodity approach to aiding in the expansion of exports from the less developed countries; (8) commodity agreements; and (9) the use of appropriate transition periods. These will be considered in order.

1. There is little doubt that the EEC was the most important negotiating party in the Kennedy round of negotiations in agriculture. Neither can we doubt that negotiations concerning grain were crucial to the success of the Kennedy round. The United States, Canada, and other grain exporters were anxious to secure the opportunity to continue to supply similar quantities of grain to the major importing countries. However, their efforts were thwarted. The Common Agricultural Policy of the EEC, which was then being arranged, set target prices on many commodities, including grains, above world market prices. In addition, Britain's precarious balance of payments position and attempted entry into the EEC militated against acceptance of any access-to-markets proposals.

No real progress was made in the Kennedy round negotiations on grain and other agricultural products with respect to domestic agricultural policy. Nevertheless, a substantial proportion of Canada's agricultural trade has been affected. The conclusion of the cereals agreement, significant reductions in tariffs on Canadian-U.S. agricultural trade, and a new anti-dumping code all have significant implications for Canadian agriculture. The Kennedy round, at the very least, brought into focus the nature of the problem of agricultural trade liberalization, which centres on acceptance by the major trading nations of some limitation on their freedom of action in domestic agricultural policies. Without this, future negotiations are futile.

2. We should not rule out the prospect for the development of further trading blocs involving two or more Atlantic countries, or among other regions whose integration might concern Canada's agricultural trade. Already, we have the example of the British-Irish arrangement, under

which free trade will extend to all commodities by 1975. There is increasing interest in the development of a Canada–United States free trade area. The possible contribution that such an agreement might make to the rate of Canada's economic growth is emphasized. It is most important that this opportunity be continually studied. It has been suggested that the Caribbean area might be included. The writers present the opinion that, given adequate time for adjustment—ten to fifteen years—Canadian agriculture could make an almost complete adjustment to free trade with the United States, but that if the Caribbean area were included, the area might require a twenty-year adjustment period.

3. The fact that farm prices in Canada showed a sharp increase of over 10 percent during a recent period of two to three years[1] is of the greatest importance. Farm prices in the United States increased similarly over the years 1964–66. The prospect that this improvement will continue over a decade is equally important, since it would provide a very favourable climate in which these countries might address themselves to the many constructive possibilities for expansion of trade in farm products.

The increase in farm prices has come about by (a) an expansion in exports, particularly to Russia, China, and the developing countries, (b) the structural changes in agriculture, and (c) the farm programs of the United States, which, after showing little in the way of price and income improvement over many years, have in the past four years increasingly affected supply and demand relationships for an increasing number of important commodity groups. This has resulted partly from the industrial prosperity of the 1960s, which accelerated the adjustments within agriculture. The war in Viet Nam is also a factor.

It is most significant that wheat stocks in the United States at the end of the 1965–66 crop year were well below the strategic reserve levels established by the Secretary of Agriculture. The following year, American wheat acreage allotments were expanded more than 30 percent. But growers, fearful of possibly declining prices, increased their seeded acreage by only 20 percent. This can be taken as evidence that, within the context of the still government-supported prices, wheat farmers are consciously attempting to plant an acreage of wheat that maximizes their returns. Acreage restrictions still exist, but they do not restrict. It is also most significant that American surpluses of dairy products have disappeared and probably will not recur. In addition, the livestock and fruit and vegetable sectors of American agriculture have for many years operated in an essentially free market climate.

[1]The increase was 11 percent between the average for 1964 and the month of July, 1966, and since this increase was greater than the rise in farm costs, the result was a reversal of the unfavourable terms of trade.

Here, then, we have in this greatest agricultural country, and the country whose domestic farm programs were the greatest barrier to increased trade, a new situation—and one much more favourable to pursuing the objectives with which this study is concerned.

4. The GATT encourages dismantling of the British preferential system. These preferences apply to only about 5 percent of Canada's farm exports to Britain. Their disappearance would make little difference, apart from providing a better atmosphere for embracing opportunities for a more constructive and positive negotiation on more fundamental issues. For Canada, the loss of British preferences on farm products would be far more than offset if the British were in a position to remove quantitative and other restrictions on food imports.

5. The scope for unilateral tariff reductions should not be underestimated. There are surely situations where a tariff reduction (without reciprocal action) is clearly to the advantage of a country. Canada recently took such action in regard to sugar imports from the West Indies. The freeing of Canadian farmers from farm-machinery tariffs—one of the most constructive trade measures of the past twenty-five years—was unilateral. And there remains considerable scope for such action. The clearest cases today are for the removal of the 22½ percent duty on dairy, poultry, and other equipment and for removal of the import duty of 8 cents per bushel on corn. Rather than being likely to worsen Canada's balance of payments difficulties, the removal of the above-mentioned duties would seem likely to have the opposite effect. These duties (and there are others) tend to worsen Canada's comparative-advantage position. For instance, Canada's farm exports to the United States are still at about 1950–54 levels, while her imports of farm products from the United States have increased by 65 percent. And only to a moderate degree is this due to increased American restrictions on imports over these years. Removal of restrictions might include unilateral concessions for tropical products entering the more developed countries. Recent literature suggests that this might be an important one of the several approaches available for aiding the developing countries through trade.

6. There is also scope for attacking trade barriers other than tariffs and quotas. As noted elsewhere, the EEC negotiators may be prepared to negotiate on the basis of freezing domestic subsidies at present levels. This would at least put the question of domestic subsidies to agriculture on the bargaining table. This would represent a considerable advance, since although they represented the basis for restraints on trade, they have not as yet been regarded as an area for international negotiation. Even between Canada and the United States there are many real barriers to trade (apart

from tariffs and quotas), largely in the areas of health and transportation regulations. These must be subject to continuing negotiation, and, in the case of Canada, there must be an improvement in health regulations applicable to food.

7. The more developed countries are under strong pressure to open their markets on a wider basis to the export crops of the less developed countries. Limited progress has been made through UNCTAD, but much remains to be achieved. It is quite possible that, for some developing countries and for some products, unilateral action by the more developed countries is the *least expensive* means for providing economic development assistance.

8. Commodity agreements, by providing a measure of price and output stability, represent a useful supplement to other means of expanding trade in some farm products. Opportunities in this area should be explored, but it should be noted that, thus far, agreements have applied only to commodities subject to extremely erratic fluctuations in price, e.g., wheat, sugar, coffee. They also require very strong support from producers in the exporting countries, and it is unlikely that this would be forthcoming for livestock products and even for feed grains.

The International Wheat Agreement (IWA) is most important to Canada, since it is the only agreement in which Canada participates as an exporter. The IWA obliges exporters to sell (and importers to take) specific quantities of wheat at the negotiated maximum (minimum) prices if market prices move outside the negotiated range of prices. Only in the first of the five agreements (which covered the period 1949–52) did market prices move outside the negotiated range—and on that occasion in favour of the importers. The United States has carried out its vast PL480 subsidized export program from 1955 to the present without reference to the IWA. In fact, the inability to include production restraints in any agreement is often cited as the major weakness of the IWA. Largely because of the large contracts negotiated between Canada and mainland China and because of Canada's reduced stocks, it was possible to secure an increase in the price range under the 1962 agreement.

The new wheat agreement should come into effect in August, 1968. It covers the principal grades of wheat grown in the leading wheat-exporting countries and will provide for higher price ranges for ten of the major grades. The increase in the negotiated range of prices is often wrongly read as automatically assuring an increase in the price of wheat. While an increase in the IWA range has a somewhat bullish effect on market prices, it does no more than confirm prospective supply-demand conditions existing at the time of the negotiations.

Perhaps the most important contribution of the IWA is to provide a continuing forum for discussion of wheat-marketing problems. In its price and guaranteed-quantities provisions, it has largely reflected what a group of tough bargainers representing importer and exporter countries consider would happen in the absence of an agreement. It has almost entirely avoided any approach to restructuring the world wheat industry on a more economic basis.

9. In any review of strategy considerations respecting the opportunity to expand trade in agricultural products, the concept of a transition period must occupy a central place. Only with such periods—and in some cases they may seem long—could progress be made in facing the realities of expanding trade. This reflects the nature of resources presently employed in agriculture, many of which would become redundant in a world seeking the gains of international specialization. This could be illustrated with the adjustments which would be required of the wheat industry in Britain and Europe, of sugar beet production everywhere, of parts of the Canadian dairy and fruit and vegetable industries. But land resources are substitutable, and other fixed investments can be adjusted out of (economic) existence in periods of five, ten, and very seldom more than fifteen years. A profitable area for farm policy, and particularly for farm-policy research, is to assess the most economic means for making such adjustments in each country concerned.

Uniting agriculture: negotiation, accommodation, and harmonization

Agriculture will continue to represent the most serious barrier to Atlantic economic unity. But with the completion of the Kennedy round and with the imminence of the full implementation of the CAP, we now, for the first time in ten years, face a somewhat stabilized situation. The task now is to provide the analysis of that new situation and to proceed to studies of the gains that might be realized from integration of agriculture in the North Atlantic area. The new situation will be difficult. After a ten-year struggle to shape the CAP, there is understandable reluctance by the EEC to discuss the gains from freer trade.

However, the situation of American agriculture in the context of trade-policy discussions is more promising than it has been for forty years. It should be possible to accommodate American insistence on expanding agricultural trade—a policy on which the United States now places the highest priority. Canada has not been particularly vocal on the issue of trade, but after observing the obviously great benefit of expanded wheat sales, she may seriously consider trade-policy changes which would lead at once to strengthening her domestic agriculture and expanding her exports.

Perhaps of all groups in the North Atlantic, the EFTA countries would be the ones most willing to negotiate on agricultural trade. Certainly Britain's willingness to face the prospect of membership in the Common Market would suggest her readiness to negotiate on the basis of a wider trading group. This study has stressed the very high costs Britain would have to face in joining the EEC. Any conceivable North Atlantic arrangement would be far less costly.

One of the most promising bases for considering freer trade in a North Atlantic area is food aid for developing countries. The need for this aid is already great and will doubtless increase over the next two decades. Again the advantages of an intergovernmental approach are obvious. Further, the UNCTAD represents a most advantageous platform from which to launch the idea of an intergovernmental approach. Under such a plan, with the North Atlantic countries leading and providing most of the required resources, the problem of farm surpluses (which have led to most of the barriers to trade in farm products) could be handled in an appropriate manner. The countries of the North Atlantic, and others, could very well, within the context of foreign aid, commit themselves to providing food in kind and/or foreign exchange resources for the purchase of food. In fact, the EEC Agricultural Guidance and Guarantee Fund in some respects provides a guideline to the approach required. Because of the priority given to grains in food aid, this program would be directed particularly to the sector of agriculture where surpluses have been largest over the postwar years. The scale of food aid requirements is of an order that would exhaust surplus production. In fact, they are of a scale that would probably require conscious production decisions to meet these needs. The ending of a surplus situation would provide a climate in which reduction of trade barriers could realistically be faced. And the systematic diversion of farm products into the aid channel would encourage an adjustment of agricultural production patterns in a manner consistent with an economic use of resources. In such a climate the harmonization of presently divergent farm policies would be possible.

The foregoing paragraphs have considered the climate, largely political and institutional, which would render certain strategies for expanding trade not only necessary from the standpoint of overcoming economic difficulties or achieving economic benefits, but also necessary from the standpoint of hoping to win acceptance at a political level. Postwar trade negotiations are replete with examples of how important it is to develop strategies that take account of the realities of political, historical, and institutional barriers to trade. When the very substantial gains in returns to resources and to consumers from a more rational pattern of resource use are widely known, there will probably arise a strong and effective desire to press ahead with strategies for achieving these gains.

V. Implications of Freer Trade in Farm Products

We proceed now to bring this study together by examining the implications of freer trade in agricultural products among North Atlantic countries. The case for the obvious gains has already been suggested, largely in our references to two recent authoritative studies[1] on comparative advantage.

In summary terms, the advantage rests in wheat, oilseeds, live cattle, cheddar cheese, some fruits and vegetables, and, at times, meats. Thus, if a move towards freer trade were made, we should observe adjustments which would lead to increased resources being employed in these areas, and fewer in butter, some fruits and vegetables, mutton, lamb and wool, and of course sugar beets (in which perhaps no resources would be retained). Because of the readiness with which land can undertake substitutions of one crop for another, the transition to a new agriculture is not as difficult as might be expected. Of course, there are the problems of skills and of the "set ways" of the farmer. It is to meet these problems that a transition period is suggested. Canada would expand wheat production in the Prairies by millions of acres at the expense of feed grains, hogs, and dairy products. According to comparative-cost studies, Canadian wheat would expand until a point was reached where the marginal cost would make further expansion uneconomic. Oilseeds would follow a similar trend.

In eastern Canada, livestock production would increase significantly, as would feed-grain production. Cheese output would double to treble in a few years, employing resources presently used in butter. Production of some fruits and vegetables would expand significantly, while for other products in this group there would be large reductions. Such reductions might leave local or regional problems of a fairly serious nature—and these would have to be dealt with on a special basis. Maritime agriculture would probably continue to decline, whether or not trade were freed. But if it were, there would be very large gains for apple and potato producers and for producers of other fruits and vegetables. The vigorous economic development programs for the non-farm sector of the Atlantic area will surely expand total demand in the region's domestic markets, and this would greatly ease the restructuring and rationalization of agriculture during a transition to freer trade. On the whole, farm incomes should rise considerably under the circumstances suggested above.

[1]The study by G. I. Trant in the present volume; and MacEachern and MacFarlane, "The Relative Position of Canadian Agriculture in World Trade."

Canada's comparative-advantage position has clearly worsened over the past ten years. This makes it imperative to consider domestic and foreign trade policies which would at least allow us to recapture the position of the mid-1950s. The most striking evidence of our worsening position is to be seen by comparing recent data with data for 1950–54. Canadian agricultural exports to the United States in 1950–54 averaged some $290 million annually and exceeded imports from that country. By 1966 Canadian exports to the United States had declined to about $240 million, while imports from that country had risen to $480 million. A part of this widening of the gap, but no more than one-quarter to one-third, was due to arbitrary import restrictions imposed by the United States. The balance represents a genuine loss of comparative advantage and should be regarded with major concern by Canadians. An equally striking measure of the worsening position of agriculture is that, whereas in 1950 more than 40 percent of Canadian exports to the United States were farm products, by 1966 this proportion had dropped almost to 20 percent. Of course, as has already been suggested, some of this decline was due to quantitative restrictions of farm imports into the United States.

In the United States perhaps the largest expansion of output would be in feed grains. This, in turn, would come about largely by freeing land now held in the Soil Bank. It is also possible that wheat acreage in some high-cost areas in the country would decline. Soybean acreage might decline as export subsidies on that crop were removed or reduced. Cotton, tobacco, and peanuts, important in the southern United States, would be little affected if the freer trade area were limited to North Atlantic countries.

The income effects of freer international trade are difficult to project for the United States because the effects of such a move on government payments to farmers and on other bases of support are difficult to assess. Again we must think in terms of a transition period, since it would be unrealistic to think of dismantling the vast American farm programs in a short period. However, we have already been heartened by the increasing proportion of American agriculture that has moved into a market context. Freeing trade would clearly speed that process. We are also impressed with the general optimism of American specialists, not only about the expected expansion of world food exports, but also about the capacity of the United States to realize rapid gains in exports on a commercial basis.

Studies of comparative costs in agriculture in the EEC and EFTA countries are not available. But there is a basis for fairly well-informed judgments. A rapid rationalization of the agriculture of most of these areas is essential if their agricultural efficiency is not to fall increasingly behind that of North America. While there are programs for structural improvement of agriculture in both cases, these programs are generally accompanied by other farm policies (price and income supports) which discourage the needed changes. However, the actual programs and market forces have combined to effect substantial rationalization. Some writers feel that in choosing to import unskilled and semi-skilled industrial workers from Mediterranean countries into the EEC, the Community passed up an opportunity to improve the efficiency of its agriculture through the substitution of capital for labour.

But the agriculture of western Europe and Britain is not to be written off. The land resources are fairly good to very good. The difficulty lies (understandably) in more than one hundred years of policies that have, in effect, been contrived to prevent a more economic organization of the farm industry. And the CAP continues such policies. In a competitive context, EEC production of fruits, vegetables, and other specialty crops would be fully viable, and so would a large livestock industry. Again in a free market there would be less, but still very substantial, wheat production in France. We are not suggesting an immediate free market—but rather that, with an adequately long transition, such changes could be effected satisfactorily, from the standpoint of the EEC agricultural industry. And considering the cost to consumers of the CAP arrangements, there would seem to be the greatest advantage to the EEC countries' seriously considering greater freedom of trade in farm products.

Moves towards unification of agricultural policies do not imply the abolition of distinctively national farm policies. It is quite proper for any country to have a national farm policy, even under free trade arrangements. This is particularly true in the area of stabilizing farm prices and incomes— a very proper area for national farm policy. Again policies for promoting structural changes in agriculture must reflect the divergent political and social goals being pursued by various countries. It is therefore desirable that any further round of general trade-policy negotiations over the next few years should include in its terms of reference the removal of barriers to trade in farm products.

At the farm-policy level this implies moving into a suitably long transition away from supported agricultural price levels that are well in excess of world prices. It implies permitting agriculture to adjust at least in moderate measure to the forces of the market. It is scarcely necessary to state again that the generally constructive changes in agriculture that have already occurred in the North Atlantic area have been in response to market forces rather than to domestic farm policies.

The pursuit of social and income objectives is quite proper. But this pursuit is a matter more appropriate to social policy than to agricultural price policy. The Scandinavian countries and the Netherlands have already provided constructive leadership in this area.

The timing for a serious review of agricultural policy in the North Atlantic area is now propitious. The agriculture of the North American continent is moving towards viability in an economic or market sense. Significant structural improvements in the agriculture of Britain and Europe have already been made, despite their farm policies, and as this process continues, the segment of their agriculture that has achieved or approached economic viability will expand. The agriculture of Britain and western Europe has characteristics revealing economic strength. It is most desirable from the standpoint of farmers, consumers, and governments that the efficient or potentially efficient sectors be encouraged to expand and thus claim resources presently used less efficiently. Just as Professor Heady sees American agriculture fully adjusted to a market climate by 1980, so we can visualize at some later date the agriculture of western Europe and Britain reaching a similar position. Such a situation, entirely new in the history of agriculture, provides an encouraging climate for moving aggressively into further negotiations aimed at expanding international trade in farm products.

Specifically, on the issue of whether an adequate degree of harmonization of agricultural policies could be achieved if a move towards freer trade were made, we point again to the belated success of the EEC in achieving harmonization when confronted with a far more difficult task; belated or not, the significant fact is that the harmonization has been achieved. As Professor Harry Johnson points out, harmonization on the level of the CAP is "far beyond the objectives and possibilities of a free trade arrangement. . . ." By comparison, harmonization of farm policy in an area moving towards freer trade, while still very difficult, would be easier. At the same time, we must remember that agriculture in general was exempted from the EFTA arangements, so that we do not have an actual example of how necessary or difficult it might be to harmonize agricultural policies in a free trade area.

On the importance of the issues considered in this study, we cannot do better than to express our agreement with John Coppock:

The real point is that an Atlantic Community, if it is to become an economic reality, should not exclude agriculture. The exclusion would not be very serious economically. But it almost certainly would become a political sore, a point of debilitating infection spreading to areas of the political body far beyond itself.[2]

---

[2] *Atlantic Agricultural Unity: Is It Possible?*, p. 207.

VI. Summary

The peculiar difficulties of agriculture in facing the large adjustments necessary to secure the gains from international specialization have been stressed. They centre on the slow growth of demand, price inelasticity, and the exceedingly rapid progress in agricultural technology. Put in very blunt terms, it is these factors plus an inherent conservatism of farm people that have led farm leaders to exercise a political influence against facing any serious examination of the gains (to themselves and to consumers) from freer trade. Rather, farm spokesmen have employed this conservatism to lead governments to establish an incredible jungle of restraints on trade, production, and marketing, to employ very large subsidies, and so on. And by the nature of the problem, these "solutions" cannot solve the difficulties, cannot give farmers the incomes they (perhaps rightfully) demand. Thus agriculture has come to be regarded as a sick industry, in chronic maladjustment to its market.

An important theme of this study is that events of the present decade have provided a climate in which the historical tendency of farmers to look to protective policies for a way out of their economic difficulties is now less necessary. Export demand, particularly for the leading farm exports, has risen sharply during the recent period. And the prospect is that the rapid rise will continue, owing to urgent food needs for famine relief and to expansion of the commercial demand for farm products, especially food grains, in the developing countries as the pace of economic activity increases. (Canada may thank the United States for converting large populations in the developing countries from other cereal foods to wheat by their twelve-year give-away and subsidized export programs.) For either or both of these reasons, the prospect for Canadian wheat exports and, indirectly, for almost the whole of Canadian agriculture is improved. In fact, it is now becoming common to assert that even if the developing countries do not succeed in achieving industrial development, but even more so if they do, their requirements would overtax the land resources of those countries which are efficient in the production of food grains.

The second change in attitude which makes more propitious a serious facing of the implications of freer trade results from the (long delayed) success which now appears to attend American efforts to bring their agriculture into a competitive economic context. Who would have believed that by 1966 the U.S. government would, in the face of small wheat stocks, increase its wheat acreage allotments by 30 percent? By now 70 to 80 percent of American agriculture produces essentially in a market context. And the proportion is increasing. It is not so much that American farm programs have been a great success, as that adjustments in the industry, largely resulting from market forces operating in a full-employment economy, have led to a vast restructuring of inputs. According to Professor Heady, we may expect by 1980 to have achieved (of all things) the two-man farm with labour returns fully equal to those in non-farm industries. American agriculture, if not yet strong in all economic respects, is very sophisticated. As it becomes stronger economically, it will surely be able to apply its sophistication to the speeding up of its national and international adjustments—much to its own profit. The greatest barrier to such development, apart from trade restrictions, is the large acreage of U.S. farm land held idle in reserve.

A statistical measure of the change in the economic climate in which Canadian agriculture operates is shown in Table XX. The greatest significance which can be attached to these data is that Canada has in recent years passed from a plateau of cash receipts below $3,500 million annually to a level above that. We expect recent levels of both cash and net income to be maintained.

TABLE XX

GROSS CASH RECEIPTS AND NET FARM
INCOMES, 1961–66
(millions of dollars)

Year	Cash receipts	Net income
1961	2,890	935
1962	3,102	1,492
1963	3,198	1,495
1964	3,491	1,281
1965	3,806	1,565
1966	4,232	1,978

Source: DBS, *Farm Net Income*, various
years.

While the structural changes in Canadian agriculture have been more substantial, they have in most areas lacked the glow of sophistication observable in the United States. But the changes have been accompanied by larger gains in productivity. And this implies that there is more to be gained by Canadian than by American farmers from an attempt to achieve the gains available through freer trade.

Data of the FAO support those presented above for Canada and the United States. That organization's index of international prices of food and feed exports was up nearly 18 percent in 1963 over 1962. It was up a further 11 percent in 1965. The volume of world agricultural imports has risen each year since 1955, and in 1965 was about 40 percent higher than in 1955.[1]

Other studies have established the fact that Canada has a significant comparative advantage in wheat, oilseeds, live cattle, cheddar cheese, and in some fruits and vegetables. Thus a move towards freer trade would lead to a significant expansion of the output of the above products; these increases would be to some extent at the expense of feed grains, butter, poultry meat, mutton, lamb, and wool. While Canada has a clear comparative advantage in several products, there has been a deterioration in this respect compared to the United States over the past ten to fifteen years. Thus while Canadian farm exports to the United States have declined by some $50 million over the past fifteen years, farm imports from the United States have increased very sharply—by some 65 percent. The deterioration in comparative advantage reflects Canada's agricultural and trade policies, and it is a matter of urgent importance that this trend be reversed. Part of the reversal could be secured by freeing the farm industry from import duties on corn and on some types of agricultural equipment not already freely traded.

With the imminence of full implementation of the Common Agricultural Policy of the European Economy Community and with the completion of the Kennedy round negotiations, a new and more stable situation faces the agriculture of the North Atlantic area in coming years. This more stabilized situation, and particularly the improved agricultural market climate which will continue to prevail, provides a most useful opportunity for a review of agricultural policies and for initiatives aimed at improving the allocation of resources in the industry to the benefit of consumers and of government— and with opportunities for improvement of agricultural incomes.

A large part of American agriculture now operates in a market context. By 1980 the industry will be entirely rationalized or adjusted to the economic climate which will exist by that date. This will also probably apply to a very large part of Canadian agriculture. European and British agriculture is undergoing rapid structural adjustments, so that there too the need for highly protective policies is decreasing.

Trade in agricultural products has increased rapidly over the postwar years despite policies which have discouraged this trend. There is reason for optimism regarding exports of agricultural products over the next decade or two. The last few years have witnessed the disappearance of surpluses of major agricultural products. Furthermore, two factors related

[1]See United Nations, Food and Agriculture Organization, *The State of Food and Agriculture, 1966*, Rome, pp. 34–8.

to the developing countries—their need for food aid whether they achieve development or not, and the further stimulation of their agricultural-import needs if they make significant progress in development—lead to the conclusion that the demand for farm products will rise sufficiently to encourage the further restructuring of agriculture in the developed countries and to make this restructured industry viable. Such a prospect affords great incentive for further discussions or negotiations directed towards expansion of trade and towards resolving the agricultural-policy difficulties discussed earlier. In fact, such a resolution of policy difficulties would in itself speed the full rationalization of the agricultural industry and so is the major challenge in the farm-policy area over the next decade or two. If an integrated Atlantic economy is to become a reality, it should not and could not exclude agriculture.

RELATED PUBLICATIONS BY THE
PRIVATE PLANNING ASSOCIATION OF CANADA

CANADIAN TRADE COMMITTEE PUBLICATIONS

THE WORLD ECONOMY

The World Economy at the Crossroads: A Survey of Current Problems of Money, Trade and Economic Development, by Harry G. Johnson, 1965.

The International Monetary System: Conflict and Reform, by Robert A. Mundell, 1965.

International Commodity Agreements, by William E. Haviland, 1963.

CANADA'S TRADE RELATIONSHIPS

Canada's International Trade: An Analysis of Recent Trends and Patterns, by Bruce Wilkinson, 1968.

Canada's Trade with the Communist Countries of Eastern Europe, by Ian M. Drummond, 1966.

Canada's Role in Britain's Trade, by Edward M. Cape, 1965.

The Common Agricultural Policy of the E.E.C. and its Implications for Canada's Exports, by Sol Sinclair, 1964.

Canada's Interest in the Trade Problems of Less-Developed Countries, by Grant L. Reuber, 1964.

CANADA'S COMMERCIAL POLICY AND COMPETITIVE POSITION

Prices, Productivity, and Canada's Competitive Position, by N. H. Lithwick, 1967.

Industrial Structure in Canada's International Competitive Position: A Study of the Factors Affecting Economies of Scale and Specialization in Canadian Manufacturing, by H. Edward English, 1964.

Canada's Approach to Trade Negotiations, by L. D. Wilgress, 1963.

CANADIAN-AMERICAN COMMITTEE PUBLICATIONS

CANADA-U.S. ECONOMIC RELATIONS

Constructive Alternatives to Proposals for U.S. Import Quotas (a Statement by the Committee), 1968.

U.S.-Canadian Free Trade: The Potential Impact on the Canadian Economy, by Paul Wonnacott and Ronald J. Wonnacott, 1968.

The Role of International Unionism in Canada, by John H. G. Crispo, 1967.

A New Trade Strategy for Canada and the United States (a Statement by the Committee), 1966.

Capital Flows between Canada and the United States, by Irving Brecher, 1965.

A Possible Plan for a Canada-U.S. Free Trade Area (a Staff Report), 1965.

Invisible Trade Barriers between Canada and the United States, by Francis Masson and H. Edward English, 1963.

Non-Merchandise Transactions between Canada and the United States, by John W. Popkin, 1963.

Policies and Practices of United States Subsidiaries in Canada, by John Lindeman and Donald Armstrong, 1961.